1970

This book may be kept

FOURTEEN DAYS

A fine will be charged for each

ORNIFLE

Also published by Hill and Wang

JEAN ANOUILH Volume I
  Antigone
  Eurydice (Legend of Lovers)
  The Ermine
  The Rehearsal
  Romeo and Jeannette

JEAN ANOUILH Volume II
  Restless Heart
  Time Remembered
  Ardèle
  Mademoiselle Colombe
  The Lark

JEAN ANOUILH Volume III
  Thieves' Carnival
  Medea
  Cécile, or The School for Fathers
  Traveler Without Luggage
  The Orchestra
  Episode in the Life of an Author
  Catch As Catch Can

THE CAVERN

ORNIFLE

A PLAY BY JEAN ANOUILH

Translated by Lucienne Hill

A SPOTLIGHT DRAMABOOK

HILL and WANG New York

ORNIFLE

CHARACTERS

ORNIFLE

MLLE. SUPO

NENETTE

COUNTESS

MACHETU

FATHER DUBATON

PRESS PHOTOGRAPHERS

FEMALE ASSISTANT

DR. SUBITES

DR. GALOPIN

FABRICE

MARGUERITE

ACT ONE

(ORNIFLE's *study.*

ORNIFLE, *in a very sumptuous dressing gown, is pacing back and forth. His secretary,* MLLE. SUPO, *is accompanying him on the piano. She strikes a few chords, gazing up at him in rapture. Suddenly* ORNIFLE *starts to sing words to the tune* MLLE. SUPO *has been playing.*)

ORNIFLE

> And I always think
> As I tumble into bed
> Of little Willie Wee
> Who is dead, dead, dead.

MLLE. SUPO

(*Rapturously.*)

Oh, it's beautiful!

ORNIFLE

Isn't it? Unfortunately, it's by Dylan Thomas.

MLLE. SUPO

(*Sincerely sorry.*)

What a shame!

ORNIFLE

It is always a shame not being a genius. Less serious though, in the

3

long run, than we think. The main thing is for the world to think you are, which is a matter of publicity. What time are the photographers coming?

MLLE. SUPO

At noon.

ORNIFLE

Double center page in color and the cover. You don't seem to realize it, but that, Mlle. Supo, means far more than inspiration.

MLLE. SUPO

(*Tight-lipped.*)

Pardon me for not being impressed. Last week's cover was devoted to Mlle. Marie Tampon—or to be more precise, to Mlle. Marie Tampon's behind.

ORNIFLE

Now, you mustn't be nasty about Mlle. Tampon's behind. It has talent. The proof is that it's famous and runs to one and a half million copies. I must add, in all fairness, that it does have quite a pretty voice.

MLLE. SUPO

(*Bitterly.*)

H'm! If Mlle. Marie Tampon was plain!

ORNIFLE

Nobody would have noticed the pretty voice, I know. But Mlle. Marie Tampon has a magnificent figure, which is already a great deal, and we should thank the Lord for giving her, on top of that, a pretty singing voice. That's what I call conscientious. Imagine that behind singing off-key: the thing would have been immoral, I agree. Providentially, it sings in tune.

MLLE. SUPO

It makes me ill to hear you talk like that.

ORNIFLE

Mlle. Supo, in the ten years that we have worked together, I long ago lost count of the things which make you ill. Your life must be one long malaise.

4

MLLE. SUPO

I have the misfortune to be sensitive. And when I see a great poet like you——

ORNIFLE

Mlle. Supo, you are positively the only person left in Paris who still thinks I'm a poet. And even if I were, it is a great honor for a poet's face to follow an attractive girl's behind on the cover of the most widely read weekly magazine in Paris. Such unwonted homage to a face is even proof—if proof were needed—of the high artistic level of this publication. Thanks to that at least, there will be, on Wednesday next, one and a half million morons who'll believe, for a whole week, that I'm a genius. After that, I know, I shall end up, like geniuses of previous weeks, dog-eared in a dentist's waiting room—or in some other, rather smaller room, dedicated to some unmentionable purpose. Even so, that will have given me seven whole days of immortality. No mean achievement.

MLLE. SUPO

(*Passionately.*)

I'd sooner die than let anybody photograph my behind!

ORNIFLE

That idea, Mlle. Supo, would never enter anybody's head.

MLLE. SUPO

(*Jumping up from her stool.*)

How can you be so cruel? You've never seen it! No one has!

ORNIFLE

Exactly. Which is why nobody would ever dream of photographing it. You must be logical. Not that it isn't an utterly delightful one, I'm sure. Put it back on your stool, there's a good girl, and let's not have our weeping fit today. It does hold things up so. Play me the last few bars again, will you?

(MLLE. SUPO, *sniffing back her tears, plays the piano.* ORNIFLE *sings softly.*)

> Young man Gaiety
> Longed to join the dance,

5

> Young man Duty
> Gave it ne'er a glance.

MLLE. SUPO

(*In transports.*)

Oh, it's beautiful!

ORNIFLE

Good, isn't it? Unfortunately, it's Péguy. I ask you, what chance is there of finding something new? They took all that was worth taking.

MLLE. SUPO

(*Tearfully.*)

Are you sure it isn't yours? Sometimes one has the feeling that——

ORNIFLE

It's only a feeling, alas! It is notoriously his.

MLLE. SUPO

(*Collapsing on her keyboard with a frightful cacophony.*)

Oh, I did so want it to be yours!

ORNIFLE

(*Kindly, stroking her hair.*)

So did I. . . . There, there, Mlle. Supo, come along now. You've loved me in silence for the last ten years and that's uncomfortable enough—but as for this grim determination to make a genius of me——

MLLE. SUPO

(*Sitting up, her face bathed in tears.*)

You are a genius! I only came to you because I was sure you were a genius! I read your early poems and I said to myself, I can't be his Muse, I'm far too ugly; I shall be his secretary.

ORNIFLE

(*Bored.*)

You aren't ugly, my dear; don't exaggerate. You have lovely eyes.

MLLE. SUPO

That's what they always say to homely girls. I offered myself to you on the first day. You never even touched me.

ORNIFLE.

You're the first woman ever to hold that against me. You were a pure young girl.

MLLE. SUPO

(*Tragically.*)

I still am.

ORNIFLE

(*Severely.*)

Supo, you are impossible! I have quite enough to answer for already. Don't lay that responsibility at my door. I'm not the only man on earth.

MLLE. SUPO

(*Crying out.*)

Yes, you are!

ORNIFLE

Wait a bit, then! Dammit, one can't do everything! I promised Machetu those verses by the end of the morning, and it's almost noon now. The photographers will be here any minute.

MLLE. SUPO

If you were to get up earlier!

ORNIFLE

I went to bed very late.

MLLE. SUPO

If you got to bed earlier!

ORNIFLE

Ifs and ands will be the death of you, Supo. If I had talent, if I rose at dawn, if I loved you, if I gave up smoking——

(*He takes a cigarette.*)

MLLE. SUPO

Don't! You're killing yourself!

ORNIFLE

(*Lighting his cigarette.*)

We do nothing else from the moment we are born. We spin it out, that's all.

MLLE. SUPO

I could have made a different man of you!

ORNIFLE

Exactly. That was what scared me. Play the first few bars again, would you?

(*She does so.* ORNIFLE *sings softly.*)

> Tinsel and plywood,
> Frail gauzes soon rent;
> In painted backcloths
> My life has been spent.

MLLE. SUPO

Is that yours?

ORNIFLE

(*Testily.*)

Of course it's mine. It's obvious, isn't it? Write it down, girl, write it down!

(MLLE. SUPO *takes her pad.* ORNIFLE *continues to pace up and down.*)

> Tinsel and plywood,
> Frail gauzes soon rent;
> In painted backcloths
> My life has been spent.
>
> O mansions of canvas
> Where fantasy slept,
> O nuptial rooms,
> Their gilt thresholds kept
>
> By an old stagehand
> Who munched jellied eel.
> Life—o the pity of't—
> Is earnest, is real.

There. That's Machetu settled, the old louse. Type them out in duplicate and send them over. I shall take a bath. I'll photograph clean if nothing else. You'll entertain the press, won't you?

MLLE. SUPO

(*Reading from her pad.*)

It's so beautiful! And you wrote it in two minutes. Oh, if you only took a little trouble.

ORNIFLE

Life is never worth the trouble we take over it, Mlle. Supo. I think, just between ourselves, that we give it far too much importance. Besides, when I do take trouble, the results are invariably labored. And I am not a laborer.

(*Opening his scarf and disclosing three rows of pearls.*)

How are my pearls?

MLLE. SUPO

Pearlier. But I think it's foul!

ORNIFLE

Foul, why? I was found to have a skin which gives pearls back their luster. The loveliest women in Paris send me their necklaces and I wear them before lunch. What could be more delightful?

MLLE. SUPO

I think it's most unmanly.

ORNIFLE

Who can say what goes to make a man?

MLLE. SUPO

I can!

ORNIFLE

Which is the reason you can't get one. I am going into the bath.

(*He goes out.*

MLLE. SUPO *bursts into tears.*

Enter NENETTE, *the housekeeper, middle-aged, very dignified, but still showing signs that she was once a very pretty girl. She brings a coffee tray.*)

NENETTE

(*Unruffled.*)

Not again! Don't be so lavish with your tears, Mlle. Supo. You'll weep yourself dry if you don't watch it.

MLLE. SUPO

(*Wiping her eyes and sighing.*)

That man tortures me! For ten long years I've suffered! But I must say, I love it!

NENETTE

With me, it's nearer twenty. Although it's many a year since I had anything to cry for. Unfortunately, it was round about the time my heart stopped aching that my rheumatics started. That's life! Nothing's ever perfect.

MLLE. SUPO

(*Indignantly.*)

Fancy comparing him to rheumatism!

NENETTE

I'm not comparing. The one took over when the other left off. Rheumatism was my second, as you might say. Only they've discovered aspirin for rheumatism; that takes the edge off it a bit.

MLLE. SUPO

Did he make you very wretched, too?

NENETTE

I joined the household as a serving girl. My wretchedness had limits, like my fun. There was always plenty belowstairs to keep me busy.

MLLE. SUPO

Did Madam never know?

NENETTE

Which one? I've seen three Madams in my time. The present Madam never did. By the time she came, he'd long since given up interfering with me in the passages. The first Madam knew, though. There was quite a fuss about it. I had to take another place for a while. Then, when the second Madam took up residence, I came back as well.

MLLE. SUPO

(*Bitterly.*)

At least he held you in his arms.

NENETTE

Oh, in my young days, you know, I never had much to say for myself.

. . . Our encounters were more on the silent side, if you get my meaning. Anyway, with my figure, I'd have been rather upset if he'd thought of other things when we were together. Besides, we never had much time, you know. I took my pleasure where I found it, with one ear cocked and one eye on the door.

MLLE. SUPO

How horrible!

NENETTE

(*Shrugging.*)

Why? It depends what pretensions you have. The current Madam with her lacy nighties and her quilted satin bed didn't do much better for herself. You know, dear, when you've spent your life in the houses of the rich, you lose a good many of your fancy notions. You soon find out the things money can't buy. Us domestics are the only poor folk in the know. I'll take him his coffee.

MLLE. SUPO

He's in his bath!

NENETTE

What of it? He's my boy now. I scrub his back for him sometimes.

MLLE. SUPO

I'd give my life's blood to scrub his back!

NENETTE

(*Calmly, as she goes.*)

Keep it, I should. His back's not worth that much.

(*The* COUNTESS *comes in.*)

COUNTESS

Good morning, Mlle. Supo. Has Monsieur finished his verses?

MLLE. SUPO

Yes, Madame. They're wonderful.

(*Reading.*)

> Tinsel and plywood,
> Frail gauzes soon rent;
> In painted backcloths
> My life has been spent.

O mansions of canvas
Where fantasy slept,
O nuptial rooms,
Their gilt thresholds kept

By an old stagehand
Who munched jellied eel.
Life—o the pity of't—
Is earnest, is real.

COUNTESS

(*Smiling.*)

The incorrigible baby! He is in his bath, I suppose?

MLLE. SUPO

Yes, Madame.

COUNTESS

How are the pearls?

MLLE. SUPO

Brighter, Madame, quite pink.

COUNTESS

(*Still smiling.*)

Then he must be feeling happy.

MLLE. SUPO

Yes, Madame.

COUNTESS

It's a good day for us all, then, isn't it? I won't disturb him. Tell him
I've gone to buy some flowers.

(*She goes, lightfooted and smiling as she came.*

MLLE. SUPO *hurls herself onto her typewriter and types away furiously.
Then she reads over what she has done.*)

MLLE. SUPO

Life—o the pity of't—
Is earnest, is real.

(*Once again she collapses, sobbing, on the keyboard of her machine.*

Enter MACHETU, *short and fat and vulgar.*)

MACHETU

Not again! Mlle. Supo, you are the weepiest secretary I ever saw. Where's the boy?

MLLE. SUPO

In his bath.

MACHETU

What about my lyrics?

MLLE. SUPO

(*Practically throwing them at him.*)

Here! They're far too good for you!

(MACHETU *reads them in silence, then says shortly.*)

MACHETU

Good. There's a letter missing. "Life—o the pity of't." Is that intentional or is it a typing error? If you put the *i* back in, it makes the beat wrong.

MLLE. SUPO

The *i* is understood. Poetic license.

MACHETU

License! The price he charges, the least he can do is not give me short measure!

MLLE. SUPO

You're unspeakable! Why don't you try writing some?

MACHETU

That's his job, not mine. I sell them. Let him try selling his own lyrics and see how far he gets.

MLLE. SUPO

But Monsieur Ornifle's a poet!

MACHETU

Poets starve in garrets and work for nothing. I despise them, but I take off my hat to them. Your boss is the highest paid rhymster in Paris. I pay the piper, I call the tune. That's business.

MLLE. SUPO

(*Outraged.*)

Business! Rhymster!

MACHETU

Yes, rhymster. A worker-out of rhymes. All the world's a workshop. Someone has to make the rhymes. But at the price I pay, I expect them complete. Suppose I took a bit of license when I signed his checks? Eh? Suppose I forgot one of the zeros? How do you think Monsieur Ornifle would like that?

(*Enter* ORNIFLE.)

ORNIFLE

Hello, you old sewer rat; how are you?

MACHETU

I wish you'd stop calling me a sewer rat—I keep on telling you!

ORNIFLE

A term of endearment.

MACHETU

Applied to me, it sounds like a description.

ORNIFLE

You're as touchy as a debutante, Machetu.

MACHETU

(*Anxiously.*)

Is that another of your double meanings?

ORNIFLE

Poor Machetu. Deep down, how you'd have loved to be a gentleman!

MACHETU

Yes.

ORNIFLE

I should have loved to be the high-souled poet I am in Mlle. Supo's imagination. And here we are, two old sewer rats peddling hot air. What could be nicer?

(*He rubs his hands cheerfully.*)

MACHETU

(*Gloomily.*)

You still shouldn't call me a sewer rat in front of people.

ORNIFLE

Mlle. Supo isn't people. Anyway, in public you call me Maestro and I call you "my dear Impresario." We know our manners!

MACHETU

It's different for you. You've got a title and five Christian names. Your pa was in the cavalry: he had a swordstick and a crest and a chestful of medals—and you told me he used to doff his hat to pregnant women in the street. He was a colonel and a nobleman. You can indulge in a dirty word occasionally. Me, I'm called Machetu and that's the handle I was born with. My father was in scrap; he'd shove a pregnant woman off the sidewalk soon as look at her, and I made my first thousand in wholesale ironmongery. I have to aim for distinction. Always the dark suit, the chosen word. I've a long way to catch up. You haven't. So do me a favor, don't call me a sewer rat in front of people. If there was anyone around who knew me before the war, it might set them thinking.

ORNIFLE

With your contacts, you should have had them taken care of.

MACHETU

(*Worried.*)

The tribunals dealt with one or two after the Liberation. But there are still quite a few about. You can't ever clean a city up completely. But now that I own three theatres in Paris—plus my works over in Saint-Ouen—I have to watch my step. Now that I'm seen dining out with Cabinet Ministers, I have to set them wondering, by the way I hold my knife and fork, whether I'm really the man they used to know. I'll give you an example. In my office, over in Saint-Ouen, I may be frying in the heat, I'll never let my braces show. None of your disherbill for me. And always Miss So and So to my office girls.

ORNIFLE

(*Casually.*)

The word is deshabille.

MACHETU

There you are, you see. It's always the little things that trip you up. I have to watch myself the entire time. So don't call me rude names in public. Right?

ORNIFLE

If I have to be polite to you, it'll cost you even more.

MACHETU

Now that's not very friendly.

ORNIFLE

Why? Because I mentioned money? I'm devoted to you. We're as close as pants and bum.

MACHETU

(*Flushing.*)

There you go again, saying vulgar things just to make me feel awkward.

ORNIFLE

A figure of speech.

MACHETU

Well, it isn't nice. There's a rude word in it and probably a double meaning. I can't get on with double meanings. I understand enough for them to worry me and not enough to understand them. I know you're more intelligent than me——

ORNIFLE

Why, Machetu, don't tell me you believe in intelligence? It's all illusion.

MACHETU

(*Muttering.*)

Illusion . . . You're trying to muddle me. What's the matter, don't I pay you enough? I've given you an exclusive contract fit for an oil king's mistress. The price I pay, I had a right to your friendship.

ORNIFLE

You'll make me cry in a minute.

MACHETU

This I must see.

ORNIFLE

What do you think of my lyrics?

MACHETU

You slipped in a license I don't care for much. I'm short of an *i*.

ORNIFLE

An *i*?

MACHETU

I may not know much, but I *can* spell. And any lyrics sung in my establishments, I want done with proper spelling. I can afford spelling, don't you worry.

MLLE. SUPO

I explained to Monsieur Machetu that in the line "o the pity of't," the omission of the *i* was poetic license.

MACHETU

Be as licentious as you like with other people, but I'm your friend and you ought to do right by me.

ORNIFLE

What are you grumbling about? I haven't written anything so good in ages. Have I, Supo?

MACHETU

(*Looking uneasily from one to the other.*)
It's a bit arty for my taste. Still, there's a vogue for it these days and that's enough for Machetu. It stands to reason I only pay you what I do because I know that you're the one song writer in Paris who passes for a highbrow. One day you'll land up in the Hall of Fame and I'll raise your fees according. Meanwhile, my personal tastes don't matter. In the old days, when there was a market for cheesecake, I sold cheesecake. Now there's a demand for literature, so I sell literature. I can't be franker than that. Couldn't you see your way to giving me back my *i*? It won't take you a minute, a clever chap like you.

ORNIFLE

Put it back yourself. I never retouch my work. I'd only spoil it. Of course, if you'd rather give me back the lyrics——

MACHETU

No, I'll take them. I'll trust the label. But next time, do a bit better by me, will you? Are you dining with us at Maxim's tonight? We're celebrating Pilu's decoration.

ORNIFLE

That jailbird? Whose doing was that—yours?

MACHETU

That's right. Whenever you fancy the cravat, just say the word. I'm well in with the powers that be just now.

ORNIFLE

I will. You louse.

MACHETU

There you go again!

ORNIFLE

In private you surely can't expect us to call each other "sir." I take back sewer rat; allow me louse.

MACHETU

Monsieur le Comte Ornifle de Saint-Oignon, I'm only an ironmonger by trade, but I'll tell you something: I'm probably less of a louse than you.

(*He goes out.*)

ORNIFLE

(*Smiling as he watches him go.*)

Probably——

MLLE. SUPO

(*Hotly.*)

He insulted you! And off he goes clutching that little gem as if it were a pound of lard. How can you lower yourself by even speaking to him?

ORNIFLE

(*Lying on the sofa with a newspaper.*)

Supo, shut up!

MLLE. SUPO

You'll never silence me! I am your conscience! One can never still the voice of conscience!

ORNIFLE

(*From behind his paper.*)

No. But one can easily train oneself not to listen to it.

MLLE. SUPO

Oh!

(*She types away furiously, in tears.*

NENETTE *comes in.*)

NENETTE

There's a young man to see you, sir.

ORNIFLE

A reporter?

NENETTE

No. Nice manners and his collar's clean.

ORNIFLE

What does he look like?

NENETTE

Black suit. Young, nice-looking, sad. He says he has something important to say to you.

ORNIFLE

(*Shuddering.*)

He must be a fan. Brr! God preserve me from the adulation of young men. Tell him to call again. I'm expecting the press.

NENETTE

Very good, sir.

(*She goes.*)

MLLE. SUPO

Why disappoint the young?

ORNIFLE

To teach them about life.

MLLE. SUPO

That boy probably read your early poems in his home-town library. He's come all this way to see you, burning with hope and enthusiasm. And you've sent him away!

ORNIFLE

He's come too late. Those poems aren't mine any more. I can't bear to hear them mentioned. When I was writing them in an attic on the Left Bank and I believed in fairies, that was the time to come congratulating me. Admiration would have helped to fill my belly. Nobody came. Now admiration irritates me. He can go to the devil.

MLLE. SUPO

But the poor boy wasn't even born then, probably!

ORNIFLE

(*In front of a mirror.*)

He should have arranged to be born sooner. Today he would be old, like me, and he wouldn't come flaunting his youthful ardor on my doorstep. *He* would have grown out of it all, too. He would be looking at himself in the glass now, like me. It's no gilt-edged security, being young.

MLLE. SUPO

But you're not old!

ORNIFLE

(*Quietly, as he studies his reflection.*)

No. Worse. It's on the way. And that's not a pretty sight, an aging clown.

MLLE. SUPO

(*Sidling up to him, breathing heavily.*)

Oh, you're unhappy, I can feel it.

ORNIFLE

(*Looking at her.*)

You'd like that, wouldn't you? Well, I'm sorry—no. I had a friend once, my only friend perhaps. . . . *He* died young and he used to say, "God turns His back on men over forty." Well, if God turns His back, so shall I. I'll be despicable in my dotage.

(*He shivers.*)

Brr! I'm bored this morning. I've had no pleasure yet.

(*Looking at her.*)

Do you know, Supo, taken all in all, you have a very shapely bosom?

MLLE. SUPO

(*Breathless.*)

Oh, sir!

ORNIFLE

(*Moving slowly to her.*)

This is what you've been waiting for, isn't it, for these last ten years? The moment of panic when I should be too scared of my own company and there was no one within reach but you. I'm such a coward. And you know that.

MLLE. SUPO

I love you.

ORNIFLE

(*In a murmur.*)

I know of nothing so tedious as being loved. Loving is pure enchantment, but Lord, how rare it is!

(*Enter* NENETTE.)

NENETTE

(*Announcing.*)

Mlle. Marie Pêche.

ORNIFLE

(*Straightening.*)

Saved! Show her into my sitting room, Nenette. Supo, I shall leave you. Get everything ready with the photographers. And don't call me until the very last moment.

MLLE. SUPO

(*Looking daggers at him as he goes.*)

That little whore!

ORNIFLE

(*Kindly, at the door.*)

The Good Lord sometimes sends little whores to men who are afraid of boredom. He reserves His warrior virgins for more important missions.

(*He goes. He is heard outside greeting Marie Pêche.*)

And how is my gazelle this morning? Come to run through our little part, have we? Come along in, my sweet; we'll try it out together.

(MLLE. SUPO *spits in his direction.*)

MLLE. SUPO

(*Shouting.*)

You filthy lecher!

(*She suddenly realizes the enormity of what she has just said and falls to her knees before* ORNIFLE'*s portrait.*)

Forgive me, Maestro! Forgive me! I didn't mean it, it slipped out! Oh.

(*Enter* NENETTE.)

NENETTE
(*Announcing.*)
Father Dubaton.
(*Enter a White Friar.* MLLE. SUPO *rises hurriedly.*)
FR. DUBATON
"Nymph, in thy orisons be all my sins remembered!"
MLLE. SUPO
(*Confused.*)
Why, Father . . . this is an honor. But you shouldn't have bothered.
We could have stopped in at the Institute. It's only a step.
FR. DUBATON
Good morning, my dear Mlle. Supo. Is the Maestro at home?
MLLE. SUPO
(*Embarrassed.*)
He's busy at the moment. An important interview. I can't disturb him
just now, but he won't be at it long.
FR. DUBATON
Are you sure? Hadn't I better come back later? I don't have much
time.
MLLE. SUPO
(*Bitterly.*)
I know the Maestro. That kind of interview seldom takes him longer
than twenty minutes. Just one small point to settle, and they'll soon see
eye to eye on that.
(*She bursts into tears and collapses on her machine.*)
Oh, I'm so unhappy!
FR. DUBATON
(*Awkwardly.*)
Mademoiselle, I really don't know what to say. . . . Is there anything
I can do to help?
MLLE. SUPO
(*Sitting up.*)
You must save him, Father!
FR. DUBATON
Save whom?

MLLE. SUPO

The Maestro! He's in danger!

FR. DUBATON

Is he ill?

MLLE. SUPO

It's his soul.

FR. DUBATON

Alas, my dear, it won't be easy. But I'll see what I can do. This little friendly visit, between neighbors, as it were, is merely an excuse. Catholic circles are quite concerned about him. We had great hopes of him at one time, when he was kind enough to write us that cantata on the Blessed Bernadette Soubirous, if you remember. Since then, the flavor of his work has changed considerably. True, there were the follies of youth, prolonged somewhat into the riper years. . . . We made allowances, we aren't prudes. The basis was sound, we thought. But for some time now, I must confess, we have viewed his professional activities with increasing dismay. We are seriously wondering whether we can still depend on him.

MLLE. SUPO

Help me, Father; help me to save him!

FR. DUBATON

Yes, but from what, exactly?

MLLE. SUPO

From his facility.

FR. DUBATON

(*Sighing.*)

I do believe that is the devil's most insidious disguise.

(*Enter* ORNIFLE.)

ORNIFLE

What fair wind blows you here, Father?

FR. DUBATON

Ah, my dear Maestro, is the interview over? Important business, Mademoiselle told me. I imagined you in the thick of things. I know what these professional tussles are. I hope you were on top of the situation?

ORNIFLE

I was. But we reached a deadlock. The subject matter was not approachable this morning.

FR. DUBATON

True, there are days . . . In those circumstances it is better to postpone it.

ORNIFLE

That's exactly what I did.

FR. DUBATON

Conditions may be more propitious next time.

ORNIFLE

I'm sure they will.

MLLE. SUPO

(*Unable to stand it a second longer, rushes out with a long, outraged sob.*)

Ooooh!

FR. DUBATON

Your dear secretary seems extremely highly strung.

ORNIFLE

Very. Has been for ten years. I can't tell you how upsetting it is for my work.

FR. DUBATON

Anything in the works just now?

ORNIFLE

Odds and ends. A few lyrics, with pretensions to the poetic, for Machetu's new show.

FR. DUBATON

And where is the great work we are all waiting for?

ORNIFLE

I await it too.

FR. DUBATON

My dear Maestro, we've bet our shirts on you, remember.

ORNIFLE

I should hate to see you lose them, Father. Back me for a place. Not to win. I am afraid, all things considered, that I am not a champion.

FR. DUBATON

The jargon of the racecourse is a little over my head. But one thing we do know; there was, in your earlier works, a breath of . . . a breath . . . that quite swept one away!

ORNIFLE

The wind has dropped a bit since then.

FR. DUBATON

The great themes, Maestro! Why do you not tackle the great themes?

ORNIFLE

I know they are fashionable nowadays, but they strike me as futile.

FR. DUBATON

Futile! I might say the same to you. It is precisely your penchant for futility that we find so disturbing.

ORNIFLE

As I grow older, Father, that seems to me the only thing worth taking seriously. When the time comes for the reckoning—on the day you are judged, or another—it will be seen that only those who entertained their fellow men did them any real service here below. I wouldn't give you two cents for your prophets or reformers, but there will be one or two futile men whom the world will revere for always. They alone will have made men forget death.

FR. DUBATON

You mustn't be afraid of death.

ORNIFLE

Don't make me laugh. You've an insurance policy; I haven't! I have never concealed the fact that I haven't got the faith.

FR. DUBATON

(*Smiling.*)

A doubting Thomas who takes himself for an unbeliever. That's a breed we'll gladly lay our money on.

ORNIFLE

Lay on, Father, lay on! After all, I've as good a chance as any. But back me to place, I tell you, not to win.

FR. DUBATON

I mustn't play the hypocrite with you. I do glance at the racing page occasionally—in all innocence, of course! We'll talk turf if you like. Let us discard our heavenly shepherds, forever willing to lose the entire flock to save the straying lamb. We must freshen up our parables. Let us say instead that the outsiders are the ones we really fancy. The others—well, goodness knows we need them for the race. . . . But we have enough experience of souls—I mean of horseflesh— to know that only the outsiders have an even chance of winning the big stakes.

ORNIFLE

Don't pretend to be a bigger gambler than you are, Father. You also back the favorite. You always keep some famous Catholic novelist, well primed with worldly honors, up your sleeves.

FR. DUBATON

(*Smiling.*)

Those are our bread-and-butter bets. Like all good family men, we never gamble with the housekeeping. But we aren't family men at heart. Underneath our robes we are adventurers. We always lay our ready cash on the lost sheep—I mean, on the outsider.

(*Holding out his hand.*)

Something tells me that we will resume this conversation.

ORNIFLE

(*Smiling.*)

And me, Father—something equally mysterious, but wholly earthly: human sympathy.

(*Accompanying him to the door.*)

Apart from my soul's salvation, is there anything else I can do for you?

FR. DUBATON

(*Hesitates, the little parish priest once more.*)

Well now . . . We are holding a little Christmas celebration for our orphans, as we do every year——

ORNIFLE

(*Taking out his check book.*)
I should be happy to contribute.

FR. DUBATON

You're very generous, I know. Thank you. We are everlasting beggars. But we are bold enough to hope for something bigger than a check. . . . Our carols are lovely, but they're hackneyed. We must wake up our young folk. If we could have a modern carol—something a little more in the poetic style of the day——

ORNIFLE

I'll see to it, I promise.

FR. DUBATON

I've left it a little late, I'm afraid. This is very forward of me, I know . . . but our festival is on Wednesday. And our boys are rather on the slow side. . . . Of course, I do realize that inspiration can't——

ORNIFLE

You want me to compose it now, is that it? Nothing simpler. Inspiration is an invention of the talented untalented. We encourage the myth for purposes of policy, but between ourselves, it's one big bluff. Your poet works to order.
(*Calling.*)
Mlle. Supo! To the piano! Don't go, Father.

FR. DUBATON

I am a little overcome, I must confess, at having the good fortune to be present at such——

ORNIFLE

(*Kindly.*)
Don't worry. It isn't Holy Mass, you know.
(*Enter* MLLE. SUPO.)
Mlle. Supo, Father Dubaton wants me to toss off a little Christmas carol. An urgent commission. We'll set to work at once. Their dress rehearsal's in three days.

FR. DUBATON

I'm being a nuisance, I'm sure——

ORNIFLE

Not at all, Father. I'm used to this. Lyrics are always done at the last moment. Machetu has a standing order for half a dozen every morning. I do them while I brush my teeth. Now, what is the theme?

FR. DUBATON

(*Smiling.*)

Why . . . the usual one.

ORNIFLE

Yes, of course; you've only the one, haven't you? What about the melody?

FR. DUBATON

Oh, we aren't too fussy about melodies. We still sing the old tunes. One the boys all know—that will make it easier for them. Something on the gay side. . . . Like this, say.

(*Singing a well-known carol tune.*)

La la la la.

ORNIFLE

(*Picking it up.*)

Tra la la, tra la. Know it, Mlle. Supo? Play it once through for me, will you?

(*He thinks a moment, then begins.*)

> Jesu, you are hiding,
> Jesu, where are you?
> I can see the kindly ox
> And the donkey too.
> I can see the Virgin,
> Joseph on bended knee,
> The handsome Kings from Bethlehem,
> And the shepherds three.
> But empty is your manger,
> Jesu, where can you be?
> In the hearts of the poor,
> Who are waiting for me.

Second verse.

FR. DUBATON

It's enchanting! Quite enchanting! Grace is upon you, my son.

MLLE. SUPO

(*Between her teeth.*)

Grace indeed! Straight from the arms of that little strumpet!

ORNIFLE

Quiet, Supo.

MLLE. SUPO

(*Daunted.*)

I'm taking it down, sir!

(*Reading back.*)

> But empty is your manger,
> Jesu, where can you be?

FR. DUBATON and ORNIFLE

> In the hearts of the poor,
> Who are waiting for me.

FR. DUBATON

(*Enthusiastically.*)

In under one minute! Under one minute.

ORNIFLE

The time it takes to sing it. Why should it take longer, Father? But let's not speak too soon. I may never think of the second verse. Never mind, I'll announce it. Second verse. I'll let you into the secret. You say the first thing that comes into your head and then you get it—or you don't; of course, there's always that——

(*Enter* NENETTE.)

NENETTE

The press are here, sir.

ORNIFLE

Oh, how tedious of them! Tell them to wait. I'm busy.

MLLE. SUPO

But it's important!

ORNIFLE

I am enjoying myself. That's even more important.

NENETTE

(*Stolidly.*)

They say if they don't have the plates by one o'clock, they won't make this week's issue.

ORNIFLE

Right. Have them come in and set up their gear. But tell them to be quiet about it. I am in the middle of composing something. Second verse.

(*The* PHOTOGRAPHERS *enter during this scene and set up their lights and cameras in silence.* ORNIFLE *waves good morning to one, bums a cigarette from another, helps brace a light stand, etc., while he speaks.*

Singing, while MLLE. SUPO *frantically takes it down.*)

> The Virgin has sought you
> With growing dismay;
> The ox and the ass
> Tread your fine bed of hay.
> Saint Joseph is anxious,
> The star has grown dim,
> Still are the harps
> Of the Seraphim.
> Jesu, you are hiding,
> O where can you be?
> In the heart of the thief
> On the high gallows tree.

MLLE. SUPO

(*Taking it down.*)

> Jesu, you are hiding,
> O where can you be?

FR. DUBATON and ORNIFLE

> In the heart of the thief
> On the high gallows tree.

FR. DUBATON

Wonderful! Absolutely wonderful! Did you really make it up on the spur of the moment?

ORNIFLE

Certainly.

FR. DUBATON

My son, I see in this a sign. May I give you my blessing?

ORNIFLE

Not before the last verse, Father. You don't know show business. A flop is always around the corner. Third verse!

(*Enter* MACHETU.)

MACHETU

Now listen, you! This morning's lyrics are all right, but as for yesterday's! Marie Tampon has put her foot down. She says she can't sing them. Oh, your Reverence, I'm sorry . . .

ORNIFLE

Sit yourself in the corner, you old louse, and keep out of the way. I'm composing.

MACHETU

Oh, are you? Composing what, if it isn't a rude answer?

ORNIFLE

A Christmas carol.

MACHETU

A carol! What about my exclusive rights?

ORNIFLE

God has first call. Isn't that so, Father? May I present: Monsieur Machetu, celebrated sewer rat—Father Dubaton. Sit over there, you, and keep quiet.

MACHETU

What about my lyrics? I'm sorry about this, your Reverence. I've nothing against your little carol, but you're not in the business. You don't know women. If I don't have those lyrics tidied up by 2 P.M., Marie Tampon throws a temperament and walks out of rehearsal. And do you know what that costs—with a cast of a hundred and fifty?

FR. DUBATON

I have no idea, Monsieur Machetu. But I don't want to impose——

31

MACHETU

That's it, don't impose. Let him do my lyrics. You've all eternity for singing to the Lord. When do you open?

FR. DUBATON

Christmas Eve.

MACHETU

That's my boy! You've left it even later than I have. You'll never take the curtain up on that Mass of yours at this rate. You got bookings for the first night?

FR. DUBATON

(*Blinking.*)

Yes, in a way.

MACHETU

Well, keep your fingers crossed, that's all I can say.

(*To* ORNIFLE.)

Do my lyrics for me, will you? It won't take you a minute, a bright boy like you. Then you can see to his Reverence. The opening is fine. She likes it. It's the next verse she doesn't care for.

ORNIFLE

What's the matter with it?

MACHETU

She says it's feeble.

ORNIFLE

Of course it's feeble! I never said it wasn't feeble!

MACHETU

So you sell me feeble lyrics, do you?

ORNIFLE

I sell you what comes in. I am an angler. I cast my line and sometimes I hook a salmon, sometimes an old boot. This is your day for an old boot.

MACHETU

My checks don't vary, do they?

ORNIFLE

I should hope not. Any fool can sign his name.

MACHETU

Father, I appeal to you. He might at least try to polish up those lyrics.
It isn't asking much.

ORNIFLE

I have a horror of polishing.

FR. DUBATON

(*Wagging a finger.*)

Genius is an infinite capacity for taking pains.

ORNIFLE

That's the way to write a classic, but not good lyrics, Father.

MACHETU

Go on, your Reverence, make him do it. It's going to cost me a fortune if I quarrel with my leading lady. You can't imagine what a
headache they can be, those dolls!

FR. DUBATON

(*Conciliatory.*)

Suppose we heard the second verse?

MACHETU

That's it! You give us your advice, your Reverence.

(*Singing from his song sheet.*)

> Sunday in the meadows
> Going for a stroll
> With her little topknot
> And her perky parasol.

ORNIFLE

(*Finishing the song with considerably more charm.*)

> My cheeks were striped with lipstick
> In the tramcar coming back
> And her little topknot
> Was halfway down her back.

(*To* FR. DUBATON.)

Would you call that feeble?

FR. DUBATON

I think it's charming—as far as I can judge of an inspiration so totally
profane.

ORNIFLE

There! You can tell Marie Tampon that Father Dubaton thinks my lyrics charming. What does the little half-wit want for the price? Not that I've anything against the girl, Father. She has a head on her shoulders, even if it doesn't operate above the waist.

MACHETU

She wants something with a bit more zip to it.

ORNIFLE

(*To* FR. DUBATON.)

Can you think of anything with more zip to it than that?

FR. DUBATON

(*Alarmed.*)

I couldn't say, I'm sure!

PHOTOGRAPHER

(*Who has been glancing from time to time at his watch.*)

Excuse me, Maestro, but if we don't take those pictures now, we won't be able to give you next week's cover. The labs are closed tomorrow afternoon.

ORNIFLE

Oh Lord, I'd forgotten about you! Take your pictures while I think. "Author at work." For once your photographs will look convincing. (*To* MACHETU.)

You're forcing me to think. I'll never forgive you. I detest strained effects.

PHOTOGRAPHER

(*Busy with his setting.*)

Your accompanist at the piano, please. You leaning slightly to the left. That's it—thinking. Look as though you're really trying, Maestro. It'll look more real.

ORNIFLE

(*Eyeïng the* PHOTOGRAPHER's *pretty, young* ASSISTANT.)

Are you new to the profession, Mademoiselle?

ASSISTANT

Yes, Maestro. This is my first assignment.

ORNIFLE

You must come again. I don't like sitting for my picture much, but I'll stretch a point for you.

PHOTOGRAPHER

Maestro, could we have one of you wearing your pearls?

ORNIFLE

With pleasure. It is one of the minor accomplishments of which I am most proud.

(*He removes his scarf and reveals three rows of pearls round his neck.* FR. DUBATON *adjusts his pince-nez in mild surprise.*

Striking a pose.)

It's a most extraordinary thing, Father. A young woman I know noticed one day—quite by chance, I may say—at a dinner party, that I possessed the kind of skin which gave pearls back their luster. Amusing, isn't it?

FR. DUBATON

Odd, to say the least.

ORNIFLE

So, ever since, the ladies send me their necklaces and I wear them in the morning. You wouldn't call it a sin, I hope?

FR. DUBATON

No. In any case, nothing quite so curious has been provided for. Under the heading of vanity, perhaps——

ORNIFLE

Oh, but there's no vanity in it. When the pearl is cured, I return it to the oyster.

(*Photo flashes.* NENETTE *comes in.*)

NENETTE

That young man is here again, sir. He won't take No for an answer. He says he must talk to you. It's important.

ORNIFLE

Tell him from me that he's very young and that nothing is ever as important as one thinks. Ask him to call back this evening. I am with my confessor.

35

(*Exit* NENETTE.)

It's only half a lie, Father. In this day and age, as you well know, we are obliged to take one or two little liberties with truth.

FR. DUBATON

I know, I know. You are—er—up to your neck, as you might say. . . . I am really most embarrassed to be adding to the general—er . . . I think it would be better if I came back later.

(*Flashes.*)

ORNIFLE

(*Calling out to him while he holds his pose.*)

No. Father, don't go! I've got it!

MACHETU

(*Starting up.*)

What, my lyrics?

ORNIFLE

No! The end of the carol. Supo, take this down!

(*Singing.*)

> The wise men and their servants
> Are gone on their way;
> The worshipping shepherds
> Have left in dismay.
> The Faithful are grieving,
> The Gentiles declare
> All hope's mere deceiving,
> 'Twas no Saviour there.

(*To* MACHETU.)

You see, that's a poetic license, too, but his Reverence isn't complaining.

> Jesu, you are hiding,
> O where can you be?
> In the heart of Satan,
> Who had stopped loving me.

FR. DUBATON

(*Sincerely moved.*)

Thank you. Thank you, my son. You have given me a very precious gift. And I can tell you, at the risk of speaking out of turn, that much will be forgiven you for this little carol, so tender, so simple . . . and, I must add, so very unorthodox.

ORNIFLE

I'll make a note of that, Father. It's sure to come in handy when my time comes.

(*Flashes. Changes of pose.*)

MACHETU

Now, then. My turn now. You needn't alter the second verse if it bothers you, but give me a fourth with a few more allusions in it. Four verses, good grief! You can do four verses for a friend, can't you? You've just reeled off an entire carol for his Reverence!

ORNIFLE

(*Striking ever more bizarre poses at the insistence of the* PHOTOGRAPHERS.)

Father Dubaton gave me an indulgence. What do you have to offer?

MACHETU

I'll double your fee.

ORNIFLE

Thank you. That will come in handy, too.

(*Yelling.*)

Supo, where are you?

MLLE. SUPO

Here, Maestro.

ORNIFLE

Let's go.

> My cheeks were striped with lipstick
> In the tramcar coming back
> And her little topknot
> Was halfway down her back.
>
> In the murky doorway,
> When we said good-bye,
> Two bodies with one shadow
> Stood out against the sky.

MACHETU
(*Enthusing.*)
Take it down, Supo! Take it down! That's what I call really saucy!
(*More flashes.* ORNIFLE *and* MACHETU *take up the ditty together, waggling their hips in a horrible imitation of Marie Tampon.*)

MACHETU and ORNIFLE
> In the murky doorway,
> When we said good-bye,
> Two bodies with one shadow
> Stood out against the sky.

(FR. DUBATON, *raising his hands to heaven, beats a pained retreat.*

The flashes continue. The poses become more and more absurd, with MACHETU *in the picture now and* ORNIFLE *joining in good-naturedly.*

The COUNTESS *has come in quietly, carrying a huge bunch of flowers. She looks on, with a rueful little smile. The* PHOTOGRAPHER, *who clearly does not know who she is, grins appreciatively at the clowning.*)

PHOTOGRAPHER
Isn't he incredible? What a character! Do you get this performance often?

COUNTESS
(*Quietly.*)
Every day. I am his wife.
(*Curtain.*)

ACT TWO

(ORNIFLE's *study.*

Evening.

The lights are low. ORNIFLE *is in seventeenth-century costume. His wig is beside him on a stand. His physician,* DR. SUBITES, *is taking his pulse. He too is in seventeenth-century costume: black gown, white ruff, pointed hat.*)

ORNIFLE

I've been rather on edge, lately.

SUBITES

Nerves.

ORNIFLE

I feel giddy in the mornings——

SUBITES

Indigestion.

ORNIFLE

I get a sort of black veil before the eyes for a second or so——

SUBITES

Liver.

ORNIFLE

And a pain in my left arm——

SUBITES

(*Heartily.*)

Wind!

(*Taking his sphygmomanometer out of his bag.*)

Have you heard the one about the patient who came out in a rash?

ORNIFLE

No! I wish you'd keep your mind on what you're doing. You'll make a mistake in the count.

SUBITES

No, I won't. Listen. It's a wildly funny story. Do you know it?

ORNIFLE

(*Furiously.*)

No! When will you take me seriously?

SUBITES

When you are seriously ill. I shall attend you when you breathe your last. There's nothing whatever the matter with you.

ORNIFLE

I don't feel well.

SUBITES

I know you, my lad. You read some medical article in a popular weekly and you've worked yourself into a state of jitters like an aging parlormaid. That sort of literature ought to be banned. It creates invalids. Mark you, it's also good for trade. I'll take your blood pressure and if it's normal, you'll do us the favor of coming to this ball. A Molière festival, you can't miss that! What are you supposed to be?

ORNIFLE

The Misanthrope.

SUBITES

You, as the Misanthrope, that's rich! We're going to have a most amusing time, I can see that!

ORNIFLE

Are we? Eighty miles there and back on icy roads just for the fun

40

of dressing up like members of the Comédie Française. While we're at it, I'd sooner spend the evening in the theatre. It's nearer.

SUBITES

Yes, but we'll give the better show. The most delightful women in Paris will be there tonight, not to mention several well-known wits.

ORNIFLE

The performance may be better, but the script won't be as good.

SUBITES

You're getting into the skin of your part, I see. What's biting you this evening?

(*Checking his instrument.*)

The blood pressure of a cherub. Make haste and put on your wig. You're coming with us. Galopin is outside in the car. He's a first-rate storyteller. We'll have a most delightful drive.

ORNIFLE

I am not going. I have a bad heart!

SUBITES

Holy Moses, I tell you there's nothing the matter with you! Dammit, I know a weak heart when I see one!

ORNIFLE

That's just it, you don't. You know about the ones in your textbooks. But if an organ doesn't faithfully reproduce all your pet symptoms, you're sunk. Suppose my heart isn't the standard pattern?

SUBITES

It's in the usual place and it's beating eighty to the minute. That's enough for me. Put on your wig and let's go.

ORNIFLE

No.

SUBITES

Do you take me for a donkey?

ORNIFLE

I take you for a physician who can't wait to go dancing. You listened through your stethoscope for precisely thirty seconds, and even then, you were trying to tell me a funny story.

SUBITES

All right. Would Galopin's opinion give you any confidence? Professor Galopin, Europe's leading heart specialist, will that do for your precious little blood pump? I'll ask him up. If his diagnosis agrees with my own, you're coming with us.

(*He goes.*)

ORNIFLE

(*Hesitates a second, then calls.*)

Supo!

(*She comes in at once.*)

Supo, I don't feel well. I won't be going to the ball. But you needn't wait. There's no chance of our doing any work this evening.

MLLE. SUPO

No. I'd rather stay. You may need me.

ORNIFLE

Don't lick your lips too soon. I'm not dying yet. You'll only be bored. I won't send for you. Why don't you go to the movies? That would do much more good all around. You may find a twin soul who'll stroke your knee in the dark.

MLLE. SUPO

No. I shall stay until midnight. I have some copying to do.

ORNIFLE

(*Looking at her.*)

Ugh! Devotion and duty. Duty and devotion. You positively wallow in it.

MLLE. SUPO

Sneer away, I don't care. I'll stay just the same.

ORNIFLE

Horrible Supo. You would have been unbeatable as a nurse in wartime—as a Sister of Mercy puttering among the lepers—a Salvation Army lassie with her tambourine, slaving away with pinched nostrils in the slums. It's not a pleasant sight, the face of self-immolation. What indecent egoism!

MLLE. SUPO

Egoism!

ORNIFLE

Yes. The face of a true egoist is bearable. But the face of you do-gooders turns the stomach. No one has the right to think so blatantly about himself.

MLLE. SUPO

Oh, you and your everlasting paradoxes! All I ever think about is you—doing things for you——
(*She bursts into tears.*

Enter the DOCTORS. *Exit* MLLE. SUPO, *howling.*

PROFESSOR GALOPIN *comes in rubbing his hands. He is dressed like* SUBITES, *in the costume of a Molière doctor.*)

GALOPIN

And where is the patient? Good evening, dear friend and man of letters. What is this I hear? Worried about our heart, are we?

ORNIFLE

Yes. We feel giddy.

GALOPIN

(*Heartily.*)
Liver.

ORNIFLE

Pain in the left arm.

GALOPIN

Dyspepsia!

ORNIFLE

Spots before the eyes.

GALOPIN

Wind! Wind! Wind!
(SUBITES *titters appreciatively at the great man's wit.*)

ORNIFLE

Very amusing. But Subites already made the point.

GALOPIN

(*To* SUBITES.)
Oh? Did he? We'd better not keep too close tonight, my dear fellow. We'll steal each other's thunder. Have you seen my cupping glass?

Cunning little touch, isn't it? I bet you never thought of it. Well now, where's this heart of yours?

ORNIFLE

(*Gloomily.*)

On the left.

GALOPIN

That's something.

(*Leaning over to listen to* ORNIFLE'*s heart, he thrusts his hat in his patient's face.*)

ORNIFLE

Your hat!

GALOPIN

What about my hat?

ORNIFLE

It's poking in my face.

GALOPIN

So sorry.

(*Turning to* SUBITES.)

Which just goes to prove, my dear fellow, that our seventeenth-century colleagues could not possibly have known about auscultation, whatever certain theorists may say. I intend to write a paper on cardiology in the age of Louis XIV. That little point will have its value. You see how all our knowledge depends on just such accidents? Pasteur forgets a test tube and discovers germs. I try to sound my patient's heart with this outlandish bonnet on and, presto, I discover that the seventeenth-century physician could not possibly have practiced auscultation.

SUBITES

(*The toady.*)

How very interesting!

ORNIFLE

(*Innocently.*)

Perhaps they took them off?

GALOPIN
(*Looking up.*)
What?

ORNIFLE
Their hats.

GALOPIN
(*Struck by this.*)
Ah. Perhaps they did. I hadn't thought of that.
(*Sternly.*)
Open your shirt. And before we go any further, let me tell you something: I've met one or two heart cases in my time; when you have heart trouble, you never get a pain in your heart. You get a pain in your stomach, a pain in your windpipe, or at a pinch, a pain in your big toe, but never a pain in your heart.

ORNIFLE
I've a pain in my back.

GALOPIN
We'll take a look then, shall we? Sit down.
(*He solemnly sounds* ORNIFLE's *heart. As the operation continues,* ORNIFLE *begins to look more and more unwell.* SUBITES *has the engrossed air of a medical student at the great man's morning lecture in the wards. Suddenly.*)
Do you know the one about the patient who came out in a rash?

SUBITES
(*Ready to sell his soul to please him.*)
No, Professor.

ORNIFLE
What a bootlicker! He tried to tell it to me not three minutes ago.

GALOPIN
(*Straightening, peeved.*)
Oh, you know it, do you? My dear man, we positively must keep poles apart this evening.

45

SUBITES

(*Hastily.*)

But our friend here hasn't heard it. He didn't give me a chance to tell him.

GALOPIN

(*Beaming.*)

You haven't? Well, a man goes to a doctor with a very severe rash. Tell me, says the doctor, have you had this before? Yes, I have, says the man. Well, says the doctor, you've got it again!

(*He roars with laughter.* SUBITES *obligingly roars too.* ORNIFLE *looks blank.*)

SUBITES

Priceless, my dear Professor! Priceless! I had heard it, but it sounds so much funnier when you tell it.

ORNIFLE

(*Politely.*)

So what did the patient say?

GALOPIN

(*Weeping with mirth.*)

Nothing! He doesn't say anything! Everybody asks that! Do you know the one about the little girl who swallowed the soap?

ORNIFLE

No! What about my heart?

GALOPIN

Your heart? Oh, yes, your heart. Your heart is in excellent shape. I wish mine were half as good. Take a bit of bicarbonate if you like.

(*To* SUBITES.)

We must hurry, my dear fellow. We'll never be there on time. If you arrive late at this kind of function, all the attractive women are already booked. I'll tell you the one about the little girl and the soap in the car.

(*To* ORNIFLE.)

Are you coming, you hypochondriac?

ORNIFLE

Certainly not.

GALOPIN

Please yourself. Good night then.

ORNIFLE

Good night. And thank you.

GALOPIN

No trouble.

(*Laughing at his little joke.*)

No trouble at all!

SUBITES

Pity you won't be coming in the car. You're missing something. The Professor here knows some wonderful stories. See you later. You'll be so bored on your own, you're sure to change your mind and come.

ORNIFLE

I doubt it. I won't see you out. Patients never do, you know. It says so in Molière.

GALOPIN

(*As he goes.*)

Yes, yes, we know our classics as well as you do.

(*To* SUBITES.)

Have you heard the one about the lobster who was afraid of ghosts?

(*He and* SUBITES *go out.*)

Enter NENETTE.)

NENETTE

That young man is back, sir. That makes the third time today. I really can't tell him to call back later this time.

(*The* COUNTESS *enters in seventeenth-century costume.*)

COUNTESS

What's this I hear? Aren't you coming to the ball?

ORNIFLE

(*To* NENETTE.)

Tell the boy to wait. I'll see him in a minute.

(NENETTE *goes.*)

No, my dear, I think not. I'm not feeling well. I shall stay at home and take care of myself.

47

COUNTESS

(*Smiling.*)

Has Providence finally granted me a pleasant evening?

ORNIFLE

Don't speak too soon. Providence never gives anything for nothing. It will make you pay dearly for your pleasant evening. So go to the ball, my love. It's sure to be great fun. And your dress is ravishing.

COUNTESS

If you aren't well, it's my duty to stay with you. I told you when you married me—do you remember?—that you would find me dutiful. Unfortunately, with a man like you a woman has very few opportunities of doing her duty. This is too rare a piece of luck to miss. I'll stay.

(*She sits down.*)

ORNIFLE

(*Bored.*)

I can't bear to be coddled. I already have Nenette and Supo, both besotted with devotion, who must fight over the kettle for the privilege of boiling the water for my tea. Don't join in that demented dance, my dear. Go to the ball. Be your gay self, so everyone will tell me you looked beautiful. I'll value you infinitely more. I am up to my eyebrows in devoted women.

COUNTESS

Georges, why did you marry me?

ORNIFLE

(*Gasping.*)

Really! What a thing to ask!

COUNTESS

It came to me on seeing those roses there. I bought them this morning, thinking that you mightn't remember. It's our tenth wedding anniversary today.

(*A pause.* ORNIFLE *goes to smell the flowers.*)

ORNIFLE

How time passes. . . . That was unforgivable of me. And what complicates the problem is that everyone falls over backwards in their determination to forgive me. Women are intoxicated with forgiveness.

COUNTESS

I imagine one of your reasons for not going to the ball is that you're afraid you'll meet Melissa. They say she tried to poison herself the other day.

ORNIFLE

If you believe everything you hear in Paris!

COUNTESS

Aren't you in love with her any more?

ORNIFLE

(*Wearily.*)

I never was. . . . Believe me, Ariane, this is hardly a fit topic for us to discuss. Go to the ball. Enjoy yourself and tomorrow I shall wish you many happy returns of our anniversary—plus one day. I shall love you, says Harlequin to Columbine, forever and a day. That's why I always celebrate birthdays a day late. Ariane, I give you that extra day! The only one that counts.

COUNTESS

Georges, would you be happier if we parted?

ORNIFLE

Really, Ariane, you're asking the most inane questions this evening! I'd be as aimless as a forgotten rag doll in an attic. What would become of me under this great load of liberty? In ten years of living with you—and that's a long time—it never once occurred to me that I might marry any other woman.

COUNTESS

Did it never occur to you that I might have married some other man?

ORNIFLE

(*Seriously.*)

I don't know any man whom I should have liked to see you marry—other than me.

COUNTESS

I wonder sometimes why you want to keep me.

ORNIFLE

What an ugly word. And how absurd. One doesn't keep one's soul.
You are my soul.

COUNTESS

I'm not very beautiful and I know that only flawless beauty might have
kept the power to hold you, once the first curiosity was spent. Sometimes when I undress before you—it happens less and less often now,
but this isn't a reproach—I feel, as I unveil this or that part of me,
the lines of which do not inscribe themselves absolutely purely in
space, that I am in the process of losing you a little more. How
strange it is, and how unfair, that happiness should depend upon a
mere mathematical equation. For beauty is no more than that, they
tell me. I am not whimpering, you know. I think it's silly, that's all.

ORNIFLE

(*After a pause.*)

You are wonderfully intelligent, Ariane. But I dislike being given food
for thought. Life is too light to ponder on. Away to the ball and don't
talk to me about my soul. That character and I are not on speaking
terms.

(*He kisses her hand and draws her to her feet.*)

COUNTESS

(*Gently.*)

Yet all Melissa's measurements were accurate to the last millimeter.
The Golden Number . . .

ORNIFLE

Yes, but there was nothing . . . underneath. And one grows weary
of gaping at perfection. It smacks of tourism. The only thing that's
missing is a Kodak.

(*Turning her to face him.*)

Ariane, what are you trying to do? Patch things up between me and
a girl I have no further inclination to deceive you with? I know we
are exceptionally tolerant and understanding as a couple. But let us
not be odiously complacent. Adultery demands a modicum of convention, remember that.

COUNTESS

I have grown used to the idea that you are frivolous, but I dislike you when you're hard.

ORNIFLE

Where's the difference?

COUNTESS

Melissa tried to kill herself because she is going to have your child. Did you know that?

ORNIFLE

(*Frowns slightly, lights a cigarette, and says levelly.*)
Does she know of a good doctor?

COUNTESS

(*Quietly.*)
When we were first married, I was very young and very silly—and I admired you so! You once asked me—do you remember?—if I knew of a good doctor.

ORNIFLE

(*After a pause.*)
I can't stand children. And I saw no reason to litter the world with yet another young rat in my own image. Why bring that up now? Go to the ball. We were sent into this world to dance.

COUNTESS

Aren't you afraid you'll suffer one day for having danced your way over the surface of all things?

ORNIFLE

I know Divine Retribution. It has my punishment all ready. It is patiently rubbing up its thunderbolt, oiling the wheels of the chair where it means to pin me when my time comes. That day I shall ask no one to shed tears for me. I'll pay the price of my pleasure. And I fully expect it to be exorbitant—for what it was. Ariane, we are sailing dangerously near to melodrama. I feel grotesque. Enough of this. The ridiculous gives me a sensation of acute physical discomfort, which I find quite unbearable.

COUNTESS

You will have to learn to bear it. I have often thought that with a little less cowardice in the face of the ridiculous, you would have been a better man.

ORNIFLE

I am as I am. We have quite enough to do, you and I, to keep ourselves amused, without sweating blood to make a better man of me. If it is born, that child will have no father; you will agree that I don't qualify. You surely aren't suggesting that I divorce you and marry that goose? It would be appallingly unfair.

COUNTESS

To whom?

ORNIFLE

To all the other girls I didn't marry, to begin with. You can well imagine that with the life I've led, I must have a whole swarm of unknown brats scattered about the world, some of whom must already be in high school. It would be diabolically unfair if I made a favorite of this one. Go to the ball, Ariane, and don't bother your head about my little troubles. I am distressed that an indiscreet word from this young person should have given you cause for concern on my account.

(*Kissing her hand and leading her out.*)

Ariane, you are adorable. You are the only woman who has never disappointed me. I often wonder why I am unfaithful to you.

COUNTESS

(*Quietly.*)

I hate your politeness, Georges. I far prefer you when you're plaguing the life out of your friend Machetu.

ORNIFLE

(*Laughing.*)

Are you beginning to love the proletariat? You've reproached me often enough for my friend Machetu's vulgarity.

COUNTESS

I see tonight, for the first time, that there is something human in it.

ORNIFLE

Now we're going to start philosophizing! How very unsavory! Quick!
Away you go.

COUNTESS

I don't feel in the least like dancing, I assure you. This is very serious,
Georges. I am afraid, for the first time, that you may disappoint me.

ORNIFLE

All because of this absurd affair? Grotesque, that's what we are!
Grotesque! But you've given me an idea. Mlle. Supo!

(MLLE. SUPO *appears.*)

Will you be good enough to get in touch with Monsieur Machetu.
Telephone his home; if he isn't there, find out where he is and ask
him to come here immediately.

MLLE. SUPO

Very good, sir.

COUNTESS

How does Machetu enter into this?

ORNIFLE

By the back door, my good lady! Why did I not think of it before?
What is it you want, exactly? Respectability for your little protégée,
someone to pay for her son's schoolbooks later on? When in doubt,
send for Machetu. Machetu always sees to everything.

COUNTESS

I don't understand. What can Machetu do about it?

ORNIFLE

My dear, the Almighty calmly looks on while we cut our shabby little
capers; but as in the kindness of His heart He is afraid that we might
hurt ourselves, He sometimes, unbeknownst to us, spreads a safety
net under our somersaults. Didn't you know that Machetu has been
madly in love with Melissa for the last six months? He doesn't sleep
at night and he's proposed to her twice. Needless to say, I took an
extremely poor view of the whole matter and threatened to punch
him in the nose. I was wrong. Machetu's attentions were the safety
net. I now propose to take a very good view of them indeed.

53

COUNTESS

But the child isn't in love with Machetu!

ORNIFLE

Pooh, that's a detail. Was she in love with me? Nobody knows true love, my love, save in the books you find on station platforms. We dance the little ballet of desire like dogs. I sniff you, you sniff me; I step forward, you step back; will she, won't she? off we go—hand in hand and happy ever after. And then, suddenly, someone—no one knows who—pulls the lead and the puppy dog who daydreamed of eternity is whisked away. Until chance, or the person who owns it, dreaming his own little dream, some six feet higher up, leads the little dog toward another little dog. Then the dance begins again, with the same promises, until the next jerk of the lead cuts it all short again a second time. That's your doggie love, and your men's and women's too. Only, this time, I am the one who'll jerk the lead. I shall bring puppy Machetu face to face with puppy-dog Melissa.

COUNTESS

And you think Machetu will consent to bringing up your child?

ORNIFLE

Why not? He's used to taking charge of what I produce. Besides, dear innocent, you may be sure I'll plan things so he will think the child is his. I'm a man of the theatre, dammit! He'll be out of his mind with delight, the old rogue! I can hardly wait to tell him the good news. You were right, it's great fun doing good. One should indulge in it more often.

(*Enter* MLLE. SUPO.)

MLLE. SUPO

Monsieur Machetu is dining at Maxim's. I have just spoken to him on the telephone. He is on his way.

ORNIFLE

You see, it's all working out quite beautifully. Ariane, be a darling, go and dance.

(*The* COUNTESS *looks at him for a moment, then says simply.*)

COUNTESS

I shall, Georges. I shall dance for the first time in my life.

ORNIFLE

(*Laughing.*)

Now you're being enigmatic! Oh, really, Ariane! You surely don't intend to be unfaithful to me at the ball, merely because I refuse to marry someone else. Whatever next! I'll see you to the car. No, better not. There's a young man in the hall waiting to pounce on me with his autograph book. Enjoy yourself. You are looking very beautiful tonight.

(*On impulse, almost tenderly.*)

Knock on my door when you come in, and wake me. I want to hear that you were the belle of the ball tonight.

(*She goes out without answering.*

He turns to find MLLE. SUPO *waiting for him, grimly, arms akimbo.*)

What is it now?

MLLE. SUPO

I heard everything.

ORNIFLE

So you listen at keyholes?

MLLE. SUPO

As I am in love with you, I consider that I have the right to do so.

ORNIFLE

Secretary you may be, but you know too many secrets, Supo. You'll end up at the bottom of a well.

MLLE. SUPO

Your conscience at the bottom of a well. That would be convenient, wouldn't it?

ORNIFLE

I wish you'd stop trying to impersonate my conscience. My conscience is a charming, well-bred girl. I have trained her not to eavesdrop. My conscience never asks me what I do.

MLLE. SUPO

(*With a mirthless laugh.*)

A pretty line in consciences you've got!

ORNIFLE

Very pretty. So let us not make odious comparisons.

MLLE. SUPO

I hate you!

ORNIFLE

That is the only service you can render me, outside of your talents as a stenographer.

MLLE. SUPO

If God doesn't do it first, I may be the one who'll deal with you, when I can't bear it any more.

ORNIFLE

(*Gently, with a smile.*)

No, Supo. You're too ugly. You'll never reach the limits of endurance. I may die at the hands of an attractive girl, but certainly not at yours. You're far too hopeful that I might toss you a bone one day.

MLLE. SUPO

Murderer!

(*Enter* MACHETU *in a dinner jacket.* MLLE. SUPO *goes out.*)

MACHETU

What's going on? Are you ill or something?

ORNIFLE

No, my old sewer rat. I just felt like seeing you.

MACHETU

(*Raising his arms to heaven.*)

I'm in the middle of celebrating Pilu's decoration at Maxim's, with three ministers of state, including, of all people, the Minister of Justice—and Pilu with a record too!—when you drag me from the table in the very middle of dinner just because you're feeling lonely. What are you, a prima donna?

ORNIFLE

But I'm very fond of you, Machetu. You're my only friend.

MACHETU

Are you short of money?

56

ORNIFLE

No, no. On the contrary, I am going to give you something, free, gratis, and for nothing.

MACHETU

That'll be the day! Come on. Cards on the table. You're in trouble again. How much do you want?

ORNIFLE

Not a penny.

MACHETU

You worry me. I have a feeling that this is going to cost me even more than usual. Come on, out with it.

ORNIFLE

Are you blind, Machetu?

MACHETU

No. Why?

ORNIFLE

Are you completely unaware of what goes on? Can't you see that that poor girl has had about enough?

MACHETU

What girl?

ORNIFLE

Melissa.

MACHETU

Don't tell me you've had another row with Melissa? I took her out to lunch the other day. She seemed very low.

ORNIFLE

(*Curtly.*)

You never told me you'd taken her out to lunch.

MACHETU

(*Blustering a bit.*)

No. I didn't. I don't have to tell you every mortal thing I do, do I?

ORNIFLE

With Melissa you do. Your sense of honor ought to tell you that.

MACHETU

(*Impressed despite himself.*)

Honor! . . . You and your big words! You can't resist it, can you? Even when I've done no harm.

ORNIFLE

Who can tell if one is doing harm or good, Machetu? Outside of money matters, you're as blind as a bat. You can't see what's staring you in the face.

MACHETU

What is staring me in the face?

ORNIFLE

(*Sighing.*)

Poor little thing. . . . I'm no saint—in fact, I have a name for being somewhat heartless with women—but there are times, Machetu, when you shock even me. There is a cautionary work by Hogarth about people of your type. It's called "The Rake's Progress." You'd do well to have a look at it.

MACHETU

(*Suspiciously.*)

You want me to put on a play of Hogarth's? He's box office death! I can't think what the fellow lives on. He hasn't made a cent in years!

ORNIFLE

(*Sternly.*)

Machetu, stop playing the old fox with me! You know full well what I meant just now, about Melissa.

MACHETU

(*A little disconcerted.*)

It's horrible, the nasty minds people have in this business. Just because I was seen lunching with her once or twice, they've been and gone and told you things. I hope you don't think I've been disloyal, Georges? Friendship is sacred with me!

ORNIFLE

(*Quietly.*)

And love? Is that sacred too?

MACHETU

What do you mean, love? You've hurt that poor girl terribly, that's about the size of it. Whenever I see her, she's in tears. In the end I started feeling sorry for her. That's absolutely all there is to it. Pretty girls are ten a penny when you own three theatres, you know. I don't have to pinch my friends' mistresses. With Melissa it's different. She's unhappy, I can tell. You neglect her terribly. So I take her out to some smart restaurant occasionally, whenever I run into her wandering about like a lost soul, poor thing. You know what women are; it always cheers them up to see a dozen waiters hovering around the table —though why it should beats me. They always look like cutthroats, those fellows—but there, everything's a mystery with women. Well, so I order oysters, caviar, champagne, all the most expensive things on the menu, so as to cheer her up a bit. She takes a nibble or two and then she starts to cry again, all on account of you.

ORNIFLE

What makes you so sure that it's on my account?

MACHETU

Who else would she be crying for?

ORNIFLE

You, perhaps.

MACHETU

But I never did anything to hurt Melissa! I've always been extremely nice to her.

ORNIFLE

Exactly. Too nice. No man has the right to play fast and loose with a girl's feelings the way you have. You've always been very kind and sweet and loving to her, haven't you? Well, it grieves me to have to tell you that you have achieved what you set out to do. Melissa is in love with you.

MACHETU

(*Most upset.*)

But she can't be! She's your girl friend——

ORNIFLE

(*Briefly.*)

I must ask you not to turn the knife in the wound. True, Melissa was my mistress. She has ceased to be for some considerable time now.

MACHETU

You never told me.

ORNIFLE

I am not in the habit of sending printed cards when a woman leaves me. I began to sense that Melissa was losing interest in me. So I gave her her freedom. What do you take me for? Now she is just a pitiful, lost creature, a poor little wounded bird hopping from branch to branch in search of shelter, and I too have tried to comfort her. Melissa is my little sister, in a way. That is why I can talk to you like an older brother now. How could you take advantage of her youth and innocence like that? How could you make her your plaything, Machetu?

MACHETU

My plaything?

ORNIFLE

Yes. Do certain words shock you?

MACHETU

Not if I understand them.

ORNIFLE

Do you want me to be even more precise? Is it true that you went so far as to propose to her?

MACHETU

(*Shattered.*)

Who told you that?

ORNIFLE

(*Icily.*)

Never you mind.

MACHETU

(*Uneasily.*)

She was crying so much that day . . . I had quite a lump in my throat myself. I told her what she needed was someone she could lean on, someone tougher, stronger than herself. . . . It was true, too! Any man would have said the same. Do you think it was fun for her—always on the end of a string, always waiting by the telephone for you to be kind enough to ask her out? What kind of a life is that for a girl? She looked so helpless——

ORNIFLE

(*Sharply.*)

Machetu, don't try to pull the wool over my eyes! When you asked her out to lunch, it wasn't only because you thought she was unhappy. It's because you were in love with her!

MACHETU

(*Sweating.*)

Yes. But I didn't want you to know, so I said to myself——

ORNIFLE

(*Testily.*)

I shouldn't say another word to yourself if I were you. Keep your mouth shut and act as if you'd never met yourself. Listen to what other people have to say. It will be a lot less fatuous.

MACHETU

(*Whimpering.*)

Put yourself in my place! I couldn't very well ask your advice, now could I?

ORNIFLE

Beginning to feel ashamed of yourself, aren't you? Let's not mince our words, shall we? Forget you're talking to me. Man to man, you wanted her, didn't you?

MACHETU

(*Sweat pouring off him.*)

Yes.

ORNIFLE

Be honest with me. Did you get her with child?

MACHETU

(*Starting up as if he had been shot.*)

Georges! I swear I never laid a finger on her.

ORNIFLE

(*With a sigh of relief.*)

Good. I'm very relieved. You see, for a girl to swallow two whole vials of phenobarbital, she must have very serious reasons. I was at my wit's end, naturally. I had to explore every possibility, however farfetched——

MACHETU

(*White as a sheet.*)

Melissa took two vials of phenobarbital?

ORNIFLE

The day before yesterday. Don't be alarmed. They brought her around.

(*A pause.*)

MACHETU

What's to become of her?

ORNIFLE

(*With a worried frown.*)

Having bungled it once, there's an even chance she won't try it again. But you know how it is when you lose your grip on things. She'll drop into the arms of the first man who comes her way. After that, there'll be another. And another. And Melissa comes of a very good family; excellent education, father a judge. An honest, upright little soul.

(*More in sorrow than in anger.*)

You can be very irresponsible, Machetu.

MACHETU

(*After a pause.*)

What am I to do? In business I know my way around. I can make a snap decision just like that. But when it comes to sentiment, I'm all at sea. I don't seem to get the knack of it.

ORNIFLE

With the sort of life you lead, this can't be your first affair. . . . It isn't for me to tell you how to manage. You're a big boy now. You must get yourself out of your own mess.

MACHETU

With the others it was different. They were only after my money.

ORNIFLE

You always think people are after your money. Don't be such a bore, Machetu. What's money? Everyone has money.

MACHETU

(*Offended.*)

Not as much as me, they haven't.

ORNIFLE

Possibly not, but a fair amount, even so. Good looks, friendship, talent —those are the things which are rare. If people ask you for your money as opposed to someone else's, it's because they're fond of you. That shows they're discriminating. You never thought of that, did you?

MACHETU

No. I have to have these things explained to me. I'm not very bright. And you know how it is in the rough and tumble life I've led——

ORNIFLE

(*Understandingly.*)

I know. It must have been a tough struggle. And I dare say you didn't always come up against folk who were any too delicate.

(*Laying a hand on his shoulder.*)

My poor old Roger, how weary you must be of your wealth! The rich think they can do anything in life, and the things that really matter pass them by.

MACHETU

(*Concentrating.*)

The things that really matter?

ORNIFLE

(*Smiling.*)

Yes. There's no double meaning. I mean all that makes life worth living. A devoted little soul who really cares . . . a home . . . Who knows? A child perhaps . . . I'm sure you would love to have a child, Machetu.

MACHETU
(*Blushing like a girl.*)
I'm not married——

ORNIFLE
A little Machetu, tough and sturdy like yourself—a touch more sensitive maybe—whom you could teach the rules of battle to. The handsome little fellow! I can see him now. Nothing would be too good for him, would it?

MACHETU
(*Roaring suddenly as the picture becomes real.*)
I'd give the half of what I own to have a son!

ORNIFLE
(*Sighing.*)
If it were only up to me, Machetu!

MACHETU
God dammit, if I had a son, there'd be some fireworks!

ORNIFLE
He'd love that, I'm sure—all youngsters do. But yours would be no ordinary child, I'm convinced of that.

MACHETU
Why, I'd make a million for the little chap; you see if I didn't! And Master Machetu would know how it felt to be a gent as soon as he was so high!

ORNIFLE
Ah well, we all have our dreams. . . . Now, off you go to your dinner party. They'll be wondering what happened to you. Go and celebrate Pilu's ribbon, the old crook. Talk your biggest and watch them eat out of your hand. You may not be the happiest man on earth, but you do have the satisfaction of knowing that you can make anyone in town dance to your tune. Next time, though, try not to be so callous with an innocent, unspoiled little creature who wasn't cut out for the rough and tumble as you were, and who only dreamed of happiness.
(*Sighing.*)
Dear God, how stupid it all is. . . . I'll see you out.

MACHETU

Georges?

ORNIFLE

Yes?

MACHETU

Do *you* think that one's alone in life?

ORNIFLE

Life? It's a desert.

MACHETU

Suppose I asked her to lunch again and popped the question, do you think she'd say Yes?

ORNIFLE

I think I can safely say she would.

MACHETU

But suppose she just cries like the other times and doesn't answer?

ORNIFLE

That will still mean Yes, idiot! You've only ever known tramps; how could you possibly understand real women? Even if she said No, she'd still mean Yes. But if the reluctance of a shy young girl to say the word is going to bother you so much, I who know her very well—I who am her elder brother now—will say it for her. Yes.

(*Holding* MACHETU's *hand.*)

I take you, Roger Machetu, to be my lawful wedded husband. There. Does that make you feel any better?

MACHETU

You're a true friend, Georges.

ORNIFLE

It took you long enough to realize it. You're such a suspicious devil, Machetu. I think that must be your only failing. You don't trust people enough. However, you've trusted me at last, so now I am going to trust you. I still have Melissa's key. I was supposed to call on her this evening (just a friendly visit, you understand) after this ball, to which I am definitely not going, by the way—I don't feel well. She'll be waiting for me. Take the key. Let yourself in. Tell her that

I won't be coming, tonight or any other night; it's better that way.
I rely on you to tell her so. That makes a cleaner break. As I never
talk about myself, naturally I am not presumed to care; but this affair
has hurt me just the same, and like all egoists, I want to avoid being
miserable if I can——

MACHETU

Georges! If you're going to get hurt . . . A friend is sacred!

ORNIFLE

(*Sublime.*)

No. Never mind about me. I don't matter now. I am stepping down.
I'll never see her again. That's final. Tell her so, and say I sent you.
She's sure to weep a little, she'll be a trifle incoherent, she may even
talk in riddles. Don't attempt to solve them—you'll never manage it.
Just comfort her, tenderly, as only you know how. She'll have prepared a little supper for us both. Sit down, make yourself at home,
even if she doesn't suggest it. She's so reserved. . . . She might not
like to. Take no notice. Have supper with her. And . . . stay.

MACHETU

You think so?

ORNIFLE

I'm sure of it. Only—you see, I'm trusting you because I know you're
a decent fellow—afterwards, don't let me down. Marry her. This time
it will be a point of honor.

MACHETU

(*On the verge of tears.*)

Thank you, Georges. Thank you for trusting me. Here, give me your
hand. I'm an old hedgehog. I always think folk are out to do me in.
But friends like you . . .

(*At a loss for the right word, he ends up lamely.*)

. . . there just aren't any.

ORNIFLE

(*A little sadly.*)

No, my poor Machetu, there aren't. You said something very profound there, without knowing it, and a bit sad too. Be off with you.

66

Go back to Maxim's. You'll have *me* in tears in a minute.
(*Pushing him out.*)
Have you got the key?
(*They go out.* MLLE. SUPO *comes in, tight-lipped, her glasses glinting.*

ORNIFLE *comes back.*)

MLLE. SUPO
How revolting!

ORNIFLE
Still listening at keyholes? Yes, this time, I must admit, it's shabby.
When he shook my hand, I almost felt a twinge of remorse.

MLLE. SUPO
(*Hissing.*)
Judas!

ORNIFLE
(*Quietly.*)
Not everyone can be the Lord.

MLLE. SUPO
Don't you believe in anything at all?

ORNIFLE
I believe that two and two do not make four, and four and four do
not make eight.

MLLE. SUPO
What does that mean?

ORNIFLE
Guess.
(*He suddenly seizes his full Louis XIV wig and puts it on before the
glass.*)
I feel very well now. I shall go to the ball. We were meant to dance
through life!
(*Seizing her by the waist.*)
Dance with me, Supo. Faster! Let's look in the mirrors and shudder
at ourselves! How horrible we look, you and I! One, two, three; one,
two, three——

67

MLLE. SUPO

(*Breaking free, breathless.*)

Let me go! I don't want to dance with you!

ORNIFLE

You'll be sorry. It's your one chance of being in my arms.

MLLE. SUPO

(*Screeching.*)

You are the foulest creature I have ever met!

ORNIFLE

(*Easily.*)

That's because you haven't been around much. I'm no fouler than the next man. The only difference is that I sometimes do what others are content to dream about.

(*Taking her in his arms again.*)

Don't you ever do something you're simply aching to do?

MLLE. SUPO

(*Whimpering.*)

Not very often.

ORNIFLE

(*Holding her.*)

I am going to offer you this rare delight. Once. Just once. Afterwards, you will be Supo again, forever!

MLLE. SUPO

(*Panting.*)

I shall have lived. . . .

ORNIFLE

Do you like being in my arms, you little fool? Happy now? Are all those knots that go to make up Supo starting to come loose? Supo, you are about to be reborn. You are about to shed your chrysalis. You may even grow quite pretty. All it requires is just one little thing. You must get rid of your soul. Will you do that? You must forget your pride and all those absurd little things that allow you to go on considering yourself human in your mediocrity: your nice clean gloves, your first-class railway tickets, your sedate walks with the other ladies after Sunday service . . . good books . . . fine feelings.

. . . You must take off your glasses and your sensible shoes and all those practical, hygienic bits and pieces you must have strewn about your person. You must strip naked, Supo, and consent to become no more than a chattel.

MLLE. SUPO

(*Breaking free and smoothing her ruffled hair.*)
Let me go!

ORNIFLE

(*Evenly.*)
You will die an old maid.

(*Enter* NENETTE.)

NENETTE

Sir, I don't know what to do with that young man! He's pacing about like a caged lion. I don't dare go through the hall any more.

ORNIFLE

He's really itching with admiration, that one! Show him in. And tell Jules to get the car out of the garage. I'm going to the ball.

(NENETTE *goes.* ORNIFLE *stands motionless a moment, then brightens.*)
Supo, get your pencil and take this. I have just thought of three ravishing verses.

> The powdered thighs of aging belles
>   Are scented with musk,
> The roving hands of their elderly swains
>   Shake in the dusk.

MLLE. SUPO

(*Whimpering.*)
Oh!

ORNIFLE

What do you mean, "Oh"? Don't you like it?

> The fear of death binds their shuddering flesh,
>   And pale love has fled
> From the rented room where their palsied amours
>   Are creaking the bed.

MLLE. SUPO

Oh!

ORNIFLE

> The neighbors listen and rock with mirth,
> And none knows but I
> That this painted monster was once a young girl
> With the moon in her eyes.

MLLE. SUPO

(*Sniffling as she writes.*)

A monster . . . you're the monster!

ORNIFLE

(*Putting on his plumed hat and repeatedly checking the effect in the mirror.*)

Why? Because of my lyrics, or because I always do, with considerable honesty and vigor, what amuses me?

MLLE. SUPO

A pitiful monster! I'm sorry for you.

ORNIFLE

(*Hoarsely, swinging round.*)

Oh, no, my girl, not that! Not from you!

MLLE. SUPO

I'll always feel sorry for you, because I love you. But heaven will have no pity . . . and one day it will send someone or something——

ORNIFLE

Let heaven alone, Supo. I'll square things with heaven.

(NENETTE *comes in, admitting a handsome young man soberly clad in black.* ORNIFLE, *taking off his hat, goes to meet him.*)

Come in. I've kept you waiting; I'm sorry. I've been up to my ears in work today. Excuse the wig. I'm just off to a ball.

(*He dismisses* NENETTE *and* MLLE. SUPO.)

What can I do for you? Do sit down, won't you?

FABRICE

(*Stiffly.*)

No, thank you. I am Fabrice de Simieuse. Does the name mean anything to you?

ORNIFLE

No. . . . Yet it's not entirely unfamiliar.

FABRICE

My mother's name was de Simieuse. It was her maiden name. She never had another. And that is the one she gave me.

ORNIFLE

I may have known someone of that name. I wouldn't swear to it.

FABRICE

I would. Exactly twenty-five years ago my mother attended art classes at the Louvre. She had a great gift for water colors. Some theatre or other held a set-designing contest for a ballet you had written. It was your first work, too, I believe. My mother won the competition.

ORNIFLE

(*Rising affably and going to him.*)

Good Lord! What an age ago that was! Ghislaine de Simieuse! How silly of me. Of course I knew your mother! Very well! How is she?

FABRICE

She is dead.

ORNIFLE

Oh, I'm sorry. I had no idea . . .

FABRICE

We didn't announce it. She cut herself off from her family years ago. And we knew very few people. Mlle. Ghislaine de Simieuse departed this life as she had lived, without any great stir.

(FABRICE *has stressed the word* Mademoiselle. *A pause.*)

ORNIFLE

She never married?

FABRICE

No.

(*Pause.*)

ORNIFLE

Yet your mother—this I can vouch for, I knew her very well—was an enchantingly pretty girl.

FABRICE

She never again allowed anyone to tell her so. That is why she never married.

ORNIFLE

(*Kindly.*)

What a shame.

FABRICE

I learned later that she considered herself already wed in the sight of God. She made it her duty to devote her entire life to the task of bringing me up.

ORNIFLE

(*With a slight hesitation.*)

And . . . your father?

FABRICE

Until I was ten years old I thought little boys weren't born with a father. Then my friends at school told me that I was the son of a mademoiselle. That caused me to change schools fairly regularly.

ORNIFLE

Why?

FABRICE

Because I was constantly obliged to fight and they always expelled me. This was somewhat detrimental to my general education. However, thanks to her artistic gifts, Mother managed to push me through to medical school. She painted ash trays for the big department stores. When she died, brush in hand, worn out with work, she had the joy of seeing my studies very near completion. One of her few joys! I never knew her anything but sad, although she was very lively as a girl, they tell me.

ORNIFLE

(*Moved.*)

Yes, she was. Very gay and very sweet. God, how absurd life is! Why did your mother never try to get in touch with me?

FABRICE

You were the last person she would have wished to see. Mother was very proud. You were the only man she ever knew. Did you like Greece?

ORNIFLE

What an extraordinary question!

FABRICE

Yes, you're right. It is a silly thing to ask. Of course you must like Greece. You went there for a fortnight and you stayed three years. Greece must be very beautiful. Mother was always saying, "When we've saved up enough money, we'll go to Greece." It must be the loveliest country in the world. . . . Its postal service must be rather inefficient, though.

ORNIFLE

Why?

FABRICE

Because you never received her letter saying she was pregnant. Which is why I have had to come and tell you so myself, twenty-five years later. My mother was pregnant, Monsieur.

ORNIFLE

(*After a pause, stands up, his momentary sympathy gone.*)

My boy, I have often been blackmailed in my life. I only know one answer to that sort of proposition. I must ask you to leave. I am sorry that your mother had such a difficult time of it. Had I known, I would certainly have done all I could to help. But I did not know. Through her own fault. There is nothing I can do for her now, since you tell me she is dead—nor for you either.

FABRICE

(*Quietly.*)

I didn't come here to get money out of you. I came to kill you.

ORNIFLE

(*Starting.*)

You're joking, I hope.

FABRICE

(*Calmly.*)

No. I don't consider it funny to have to kill someone. But there it is.

I swore a solemn oath when I was ten years old. And I am not in the habit of breaking my word.

(*Changing his tone.*)

Take off your wig. You look absurd. I can't kill you looking like that.

ORNIFLE

(*Bearing down on him, furious.*)

Why, you idiotic little pipsqueak! I'll box your ears for you in a minute! How dare you come bursting into a private house and making a scene like this? Anyway, this is utterly ridiculous! I seduced your mother, right! She had a child, right! But that was twenty-five years ago! What do you think you're playing at? Dropping in out of nowhere like a meteorite a quarter of a century later!

FABRICE

I hadn't your address. I never even knew your name till Mother died.

ORNIFLE

To begin with, what makes you so sure that your mother had no other man but me in twenty-five years?

FABRICE

(*Quietly.*)

Honor. Mother was a very honorable person. And I told you, she considered herself married in the sight of God.

ORNIFLE

(*With a short laugh.*)

Honor . . . honor . . . That's too easy!

FABRICE

(*With comic earnestness.*)

No. It's difficult. Damned difficult, believe me. Do you think I've nothing better to do in life than kill you! I am engaged to be married and I still have some exams to sit for.

ORNIFLE

(*Taking his arm.*)

Well then, my boy, you'll do me the favor of getting married first, which is always a good thing. After that, you will sit for your exams and put these crazy fancies right out of your head. Do you need any money?

74

FABRICE

No.

ORNIFLE

What do you need, then?

FABRICE

(*As simply as possible.*)

Honor. Step back a bit. I don't want to kill you point-blank. And take off your wig. I don't want you to look silly when you're dead, either. After all, you are my father.

(*Shouting.*)

Take your wig off, will you! It's in your own interests. I can't wait any longer. Will you take it off or won't you? All right then, I shall kill you as you are. If you want to look ridiculous, that's your affair. (*He pulls a revolver out of his pocket, aims at* ORNIFLE, *and pulls the trigger. The gun fails to go off. He tries again, nervously. Another click.* ORNIFLE *watches him without moving. Then, all of a sudden, he collapses.*

Yelling.)

Wait a minute! I haven't fired yet!

(*Looking at his gun.*)

What on earth happened to those bullets? This is another of Marguerite's tricks!

(*He throws down his gun in a rage. Then, seeing* ORNIFLE *lying inanimate on the floor, he mutters.*)

That fellow has a weak heart.

(*He picks up* ORNIFLE; *lays him on the couch; listens for some time to his heart; pulls a small book out of his pocket; consults it; replaces it; takes it out again, uncertain; and finally concludes.*)

Retraction of the left ventricle. Mitral stenosis. Intermittent tachycardia. Bishop's disease. No doubt about it. Lucky for him I'm a doctor. There's some oil of camphor in my bag. Now where did I leave the thing? In the hall. . . . I'll give him an injection.

(*He goes out, picking up his gun.* ORNIFLE *remains on the couch.*

MLLE. SUPO *comes in. She is entirely naked save for a tablecloth fancifully draped about her person.*)

   MLLE. SUPO

(*Standing very straight in the doorway, ready for the sacrificial altar.*)
I accept. I am a chattel.

(ORNIFLE, *lying on the sofa, does not stir, and with good reason.*)

ACT THREE

(ORNIFLE's *bedroom*.

He is lying in bed center stage, propped up with pillows and sur-rounded by his family and familiars. The scene is very reminiscent of "The Last Hours of Louis XIV.")

ORNIFLE

(*Tenderly, contemplating* FABRICE.)

Dear little lad. . . . How old did you say you were when you made up your mind to kill me?

FABRICE

Ten.

ORNIFLE

How admirable! A little justice-loving prodigy of ten! I love promising children. And did you never go back on your decision?

FABRICE

Never. An oath is an oath.

ORNIFLE

You hear that, Machetu?

MACHETU

Yes.

ORNIFLE

There's honor for you.

MACHETU

Yes.

ORNIFLE

I want you to take notes. Have you a pencil?

(MACHETU *searches frantically through his pockets for a pencil without success.*)

It is good that the sense of honor should be lively in the young, even if the consequences are at times unpleasant. Honor is honor. Do you understand, Machetu?

MACHETU

Yes, Georges.

ORNIFLE

Put it down, then.

(MACHETU *again hunts for a pencil, for the look of the thing, then gives up.*

Turning to FABRICE.)

Now, my boy, go and fetch your fiancée. You really shouldn't have left her to freeze to death in the car. The poor child must be dreadfully worried at your taking such an age to kill me. Go and get her. I want to give you my blessing.

(*He makes a majestic gesture of dismissal.* FABRICE *goes out.* ORNIFLE *turns to the others, with all the ease in the world, and speaks confidentially.*)

I hear she's absolutely ravishing. I can't wait to see her. I mean to marry them and set them up in life. How good it feels to be good! And how easy! Why did I never think of it before? My friends, I have behaved very reprehensibly toward you all. Yes, I have. Don't protest.

(*Looking at them.*)

Not that you are, I notice. I mean this chiefly for you, Ariane.

COUNTESS

Don't tire yourself, Georges, please. Your doctors have promised to come as soon as the ball is over.

ORNIFLE

They will merely confirm a diagnosis I suspected long ago. I seemed to be seeing you all from such a long way off. I couldn't think why I felt so light, suddenly . . . a soap bubble, a breath of wind. . . . I know why now. I was no longer of this world.

COUNTESS

Georges! They listened to your heart only last night.

ORNIFLE

You don't know those fellows. Here am I with one foot in the grave and all they can think about is having fun. A fancy-dress ball! Lord, how futile men can be! Have you ever read Pascal, Machetu?

MACHETU

Pascal who?

ORNIFLE

Pascal period.

MACHETU

(*Hesitantly.*)

N—no.

ORNIFLE

You must. Make a note of the name.

(MACHETU *makes another halfhearted attempt to find a pencil.*)

COUNTESS

Be sensible, Georges. The boy admitted that he was only in his third year. His diagnosis is bound to be unreliable——

ORNIFLE

No, no. He showed me it all in his little book.

(*Brings it out from under his pillow.*)

I am keeping it by me in order to confound old Galopin. *Essentials of Medicine* by Debove and Salard. Good little book, this. It's useful, it fits into the breast pocket and it lists all the possible ways of dying. You can take your choice. Page 164. I marked the place.

(*Reading.*)

"Mitral stenosis. Retraction of the left ventricle. Intermittent tachy-
cardia." All my symptoms. It's Bishop's disease all right. The galloping
kind. There's a slow variety too, but I have opted for the other. It's
more me.
(*Reading.*)
"Extremities bluish."
(*He looks at his fingers.* MACHETU *looks too.*)
Are my fingers blue?

MACHETU

Yellow, I should say.

ORNIFLE

I smoke too much. It would almost have been better if they had been
blue.

MACHETU

Is it bad to smoke?

ORNIFLE

It's bad to do a lot of things, my poor Machetu. If I survive this
attack, we shall have to revise our entire lives, you and I.
(*Reading.*)
"Eyes dull."
(*He turns his eyes toward* MACHETU.)

MACHETU

More on the bright side, if you ask me.

ORNIFLE

That's worse. It says here, bottom of page 165: "The attack may be
attended by a marked increase in temperature." You ought to buy
this little book, Machetu. It would temper your brash desire for bustle
and good health. How do you feel? You look seedy. Any pain at all?

MACHETU

(*Quickly.*)
No. I feel fine.

ORNIFLE

That doesn't mean anything. I feel fine too. As a matter of fact, I
never felt better in my life. But that, it seems, is a very bad sign.

COUNTESS

(*Near breaking point.*)

Georges! Please! Stop this play-acting! I can't bear it!

ORNIFLE

(*Very kindly.*)

My dear, no sighs, no tears—our life together has been the lightest of light comedies. Let us keep the gossamer touch.

COUNTESS

At least wait until Subites and Galopin have examined you.

ORNIFLE

Ariane, just because it appears that I am no longer as well as I used to be, the last thing we want is a tearful deathbed scene. It would be in the worst of taste and to the very last I mean to avoid errors of taste—the only errors, incidentally, I have ever been at pains to shun. But I have done a lot of thinking—

(*He smiles.*)

—in the last two hours. Let me not boast. . . . You are the only human being I have ever loved.

COUNTESS

(*Gently.*)

Ought I to say Thank you, Georges?

ORNIFLE

(*Suddenly.*)

Mlle. Ariane de Saint-Loup, will you be my wife?

COUNTESS

Yes, Monsieur.

ORNIFLE

And off I went with that willowy girl, that youthful stranger who still yearned for the moon—full of high resolutions. I must have made you very unhappy.

COUNTESS

(*Gently.*)

No, Georges, not unhappy, exactly. Bewildered.

ORNIFLE

Bewildered?

COUNTESS

Yes. You could be all things in one, Georges, the best of men and the worst, too, by turns or all at once, sometimes, if the fancy took you—and it left me a little dazed. . . . I have been trotting around this house for ten years, pouring tea for our friends, giving orders to the servants, conscientiously buying all the dresses necessary to go on looking pretty . . . and smiling all the time—my cheeks ache with it at night before I go to bed—without ever daring to clasp my arms around something tangible for fear of catching nothing but the empty air. It's a curious sensation, you know, after a while.

ORNIFLE

Ariane, don't——

COUNTESS

(*With a smile.*)

So many women must have nagged you, Georges. My reproaches are really very mild.

ORNIFLE

They are to the point. That's why they frighten me. I am used to hysterics and frenzied accusations. It takes scratch marks on the face and suicide attempts to reassure me.

(*He becomes serious again and says quietly.*)

I'll tell you something, though. Something charming, which you may take well or badly—one never knows with your sex—but you are the only woman I did not take for my pleasure.

COUNTESS

(*After a pause.*)

I take it well, Georges.

ORNIFLE

(*Lightly.*)

What did you do with my soul, Ariane?—you who are always so tidy. I have a feeling that I left it with you in the early days of our marriage, some ten years ago, one day when I was finding it a little cumbersome. Could I have it back a second? I may need it shortly.

COUNTESS

(*After a slight pause.*)

I am afraid that you might frighten it now. It has grown very un-
accustomed to you.

ORNIFLE

(*Keeping up the game, a little anxiously.*)

And yours? How is yours keeping? You had a sweet one, I seem to
recall.

COUNTESS

(*With a quiet smile.*)

It died, Georges.

ORNIFLE

(*Lightly, avoiding her eyes.*)

No, did it? What of, poor thing?

COUNTESS

(*In a whisper, but still faintly smiling.*)

Starvation.

(*A short pause.* ORNIFLE *looks at them all and murmurs.*)

ORNIFLE

Would you believe it? What frail little creatures they are! So you all
had souls! Even Supo! Even Machetu!

(*He looks at* MACHETU, *who is growing more and more embarrassed.*)

So you had a soul all along and you never said a word about it?

MACHETU

Er, I——

ORNIFLE

Well, I'll be damned. Where did you keep it? We never saw a sign
of it.

MACHETU

You know how it is in business. . . .

ORNIFLE

We shall have to take it seriously in hand if I come through this
safely. We've our work cut out, Machetu, you and I. I gave you a key
tonight. Of course there's no question of your using it now. Give
it back to me.

(MACHETU *hesitates; then, under* ORNIFLE's *stern gaze, he feels in his pocket and produces the key.* ORNIFLE *puts it under his pillow.*)
Thank you.

ORNIFLE

MACHETU

Are you . . . keeping it for yourself?

ORNIFLE

We'll see. First we must set our house in order. Then, when we've tidied up a little, we'll see what's to be done.
(*Seriously.*)
I suppose it never crossed your mind that the owner of that key might have one too?

MACHETU

A key?

ORNIFLE

No, a soul, you fool.
(*Enter* FABRICE, *alone. He hovers in the doorway, at a loss.*)
Alone?
(FABRICE *continues to stand there dumbly.*)
Well? Say something! Are you dumb? Where is she?
(FABRICE *hesitates, then drops into the nearest armchair, sobbing.*)

FABRICE

She's gone!

ORNIFLE

Well, really! As if we hadn't enough trouble! Pull yourself together, my boy.
(*To the others.*)
Look after him! Don't just stand there! Comfort him! You know I'm not allowed to move!

COUNTESS

(*Going to* FABRICE.)
Sir——

ORNIFLE

(*Yelling at her.*)
Don't call him "sir!" He'll think something real is happening to him. Offer him a candy bar!

FABRICE

(*Rising to his feet, his feelings hurt.*)
I think I had better go——

ORNIFLE

Now, my boy, don't panic. It's clear you're only a beginner. She went because it was cold in the car or she was quite simply bored. Women can't bear to be kept waiting. That's a torment they reserve for us.

FABRICE

No. It's worse than that. Marguerite has gone for good. She left me a letter on the windshield.
(*He produces it.*)

ORNIFLE

(*Grabbing it.*)
Show me.
(*He runs his eyes over the letter.*)
My poor boy, this is a very sweet letter. She says she loathes you. In proper farewell notes you say you'll always be good friends and you never meet again. If she hates you, you'll see her tomorrow.

FABRICE

(*Stubbornly.*)
No, I shan't. Tomorrow she'll be gone.

ORNIFLE

Oh?

FABRICE

To South Africa.

ORNIFLE

The situation is really getting out of hand! Where the devil did you pick up a girl who at the slightest hitch goes off sulking to South Africa?

FABRICE

Her father didn't want her to marry me.

ORNIFLE

I'm sorry about that. I should have liked to give her my blessing.

JEAN ANOUILH

FABRICE

I won't bother you any longer. . . . I'm sorry for all the trouble I caused this evening. I suppose it must have been absurd, turning up after twenty-five years, brandishing a gun . . . that wasn't even loaded. Marguerite was right, I'm sure. She'll like it in South Africa. Look after yourself. Get well soon. Tell your doctors that I merely gave you a shot of camphorated oil. It appears to have relieved the immediate effects of the attack. That's a good sign. After all, I may have been wrong about that too.

(*He turns to go. As he opens the door, he falls in a dead faint.*)

ORNIFLE

Oh, no! Don't tell me he's a heart case too! Fate is upon us! We are acting a Greek tragedy! Lay him on the sofa! Eau de Cologne! Iodine! Penicillin! Do something! Lay him flat, for God's sake! Supo, hold him properly! I know it's new to you, but a man isn't that heavy! Loosen his tie, open his shirt! Nenette, you do it. It won't scare *you,* I know. . . . Ariane, take over from that idiot girl, will you. Dammit, *I* can't help. If I lift a finger, you'll have two corpses on your hands. Machetu, fetch a spare doctor. No, let's not do anything rash. Where's that little book? Let's see what's the matter with him. Machetu, look it up, will you.

MACHETU

(*Taking the book.*)

What section?

ORNIFLE

Doctors' diseases. Nenette, look in his bag. There may be a bit more oil of camphor. It seems to be good for most things.

(NENETTE *looks inside the bag and drops it with a scream.*)

What's the matter?

NENETTE

There's a gun in it!

ORNIFLE

(*Who has got out of bed, unthinkingly.*)

It isn't loaded. But give it to me in case the young fool takes it into his head to use it when he gets home. Poor little chap! Now that he needn't play the man any more, he doesn't look a day over twelve. When you come to think of it, it's charming, having a son.

(*Turning to* MACHETU, *sternly.*)

Machetu, remind me that I want to talk to you. . . .

(*Fuming.*)

The little bitch! I'll give her South Africa! . . . He's coming around!

FABRICE

I'm so sorry.

ORNIFLE

I wish you wouldn't keep saying "sorry." It's most irritating. Is it your heart? What page is it in that little book of yours?

FABRICE

(*Smiling.*)

No. How stupid of me. . . . It's only a faint. The excitement . . . I missed my dinner. . . .

ORNIFLE

It doesn't take much to make you pass out, does it?

FABRICE

Well, you see, I . . . haven't eaten anything for two days. I'm rather hard-up at the moment——

ORNIFLE

(*Turning on her in fury.*)

Nenette, what are you waiting for?

(NENETTE *goes out hurriedly.*

Grumbling.)

No food for two days because he hadn't any money. . . . Machetu, aren't you ashamed? Not to mention killing his dad. That's no joke on an empty stomach. Did Marguerite know that?

FABRICE

No, of course not. She has her meals at home.

ORNIFLE

(*Purple with indignation.*)

Milady takes her meals at home. Milady has a plane ticket for South

Africa in her purse and threatens to make use of it at the drop of a
hat! She lets my son collapse from malnutrition among total strangers!
What kind of a girl is this! Machetu, help him into a chair. . . .
Clear that little table there. We'll feast him on foie gras and champagne, bless his heart. That's a sight more effective than camphorated
oil.

MACHETU

(*Helping* ORNIFLE.)

It must be a craze with the girls just now. Pilu was telling me only
this evening, his daughter's off to South Africa as well.

ORNIFLE

(*Shaking off* MACHETU *and leaping over to* FABRICE.)

Good God! What's Marguerite's other name?

FABRICE

Pilu.

ORNIFLE

(*Drawing himself up to his full height and looking sternly at*
MACHETU.)

Machetu!

MACHETU

(*Uneasily.*)

Yes?

ORNIFLE

(*Dangerously calm.*)

Does that jailbird Pilu refuse to let his daughter marry my son?

MACHETU

(*On hot bricks.*)

I don't know, I . . . Look, Georges, man to man, let's be realistic
about this. I don't think you quite realize how big Pilu is these days.
Apart from his fruit-growing concerns, there's the newspaper—and
the cement combine. We drank to his first million only last year. And
for Pilu to admit to a million——

ORNIFLE

What do I care about his millions? Go and tell him that his daughter can't have my son. I'm not having an ex-convict in my family. He has a police record, your precious Pilu!

MACHETU

Yes, but as from this evening he's got the Legion of Honor.

ORNIFLE

(*Contemptuously.*)

It takes more than a scrap of red ribbon to cover up a dirty past. He'll need a full-sized cravat for that.

MACHETU

(*Genuinely shocked.*)

Georges! That's no way to talk of the Legion of Honor! Is nothing sacred to you?

ORNIFLE

(*Terrible in his anger.*)

Yes! Love! The honor of young men of good family! Machetu, get into your car—your ridiculous van of a car, which you can never manage to park—and drive like fury. Go and tell your pal Pilu that his daughter has seduced my son, and bring her back here immediately!

MACHETU

But Georges! I don't think you quite realize the sort of man Pilu is!

ORNIFLE

(*Quite unimpressed.*)

Machetu, in the years that we have been—as I said before, rather to your dismay—as close as pants and bum, I have had occasion to learn quite a bit about you—almost as much, I should say, as you know about your friend Pilu. I smile at your shabby little antics, I drink your champagne at Maxim's, I even borrow from you on occasion; but don't force me to have to teach you that there is something even more implacable than your cutthroat gangsterdom, and that is the freemasonry of honorable men.

MACHETU

(*Daunted.*)

There you go again with your big words. . . . But look here, you must admit, a million is a million——

ORNIFLE

You poor devil! You and your money, how it can dazzle you! Give me that million of yours and see if I don't blow the lot in eighteen months.

(*With a superb gesture.*)

Fetch me Pilu's daughter!

MACHETU

(*With a shamefaced snigger.*)

Very good, your Grace.

ORNIFLE

And hurry, there's a good fellow.

(MACHETU *goes, shrugging his shoulders a good ten times to show he is no fool.*)

FABRICE

(*Holding his head in his hands and moaning.*)

Her father's consent is nothing. You don't know Marguerite!

ORNIFLE

No. But I have known quite a few other women. Leave everything to me.

(*Rubbing his hands in glee.*)

What fun it is to think of other people for a change! Well, Ariane, happy now? It's the hearts and flowers department here this evening. Romeo and Juliet. It makes a change from our usual repertoire. You'd hardly know me, would you?

COUNTESS

I have just met a young man I once knew very well, years ago.

ORNIFLE

The devil you have! And I suppose you're going to tell me that you've played me false with him?

COUNTESS

The first two months of our marriage, yes, Georges. Then, he died. And ever since, without knowing it, you have been living with his widow.

ORNIFLE

May she be merry! The prodigal son is returned! We'll dine off fatted calf every day of the week as of tonight. Until you loathe the very sight of it, my dear. . . . Ariane, why don't you lie down for a while? I have made you spend an abominable night. Galopin and Subites will dance the last waltz before coming to find out if I'm dead or not. I know them.

(*The* COUNTESS *goes.* NENETTE *comes in with a tray, which she sets before* FABRICE. ORNIFLE *bundles* MLLE. SUPO *out of the room.*)

Back to your keyhole, Supo! For once, you'll have an edifying scene to listen to.

(MLLE. SUPO *goes.*

To FABRICE.)

Now then, my lad, to business. Now that we know a bit about each other, we have an account to settle, you and I. . . . Dig into that foie gras and help yourself to champagne.

FABRICE

(*Stiffly.*)

No, thank you. I never touch wine or spirits.

ORNIFLE

I'll overlook the spirits. But it's sad about the wine. I'll win you around to it.

FABRICE

Marguerite already tried. But from the days when I first went along with friends, at the age of fifteen, I swore a solemn oath to Mother that I should never attempt to drown my sorrows in drink.

ORNIFLE

Your life seems to have been curiously strewn with oaths.

FABRICE

Yes, it has.

ORNIFLE

(*Kindly, pouring himself some champagne.*)

You know, before you drown, you can do a fair amount of sailing. And not all sea captains run aground, my boy.

FABRICE

It won't do you any good either, you know, in your condition.

ORNIFLE

(*Simply.*)

Just one glass, Doctor. It's depressing enough having to die, without stinting oneself into the bargain.

(ORNIFLE *looks at him over the rim of his glass and bursts into a long, good-natured laugh.*)

FABRICE

(*On the defensive.*)

What's the matter?

ORNIFLE

I'm looking at you. I am titillating my paternal instinct. It's one of the few pleasures I have never tasted. I am trying to visualize that little boy whom I shall never see. To think I never taught you to play marbles!

FABRICE

I was never very good at marbles.

ORNIFLE

Exactly, that's the pity of it—I was sensational. I would have passed on all my tips. I am going to have so many useful tips to give you. I feel as wise as an old mountain beside you. You look so tense and so vulnerable. . . . It's difficult, isn't it, being a man?

FABRICE

Yes.

ORNIFLE

Now a girl has hardly anything to learn. You don't teach water how to flow. But a little man, who thinks he has to tilt at every windmill . . . And here I am, meeting you for the first time, on the day of your first real sorrow. Never mind, we'll start with the end of the course. I'll teach you the most important thing. I'll teach you how not to get hurt.

FABRICE

(*Stiff and suspicious.*)

I am not afraid of getting hurt.

ORNIFLE

No, of course not. You'd be contemptible if you were. But if you only knew the time one wastes over it!

FABRICE

(*Hostile.*)

And how not to hurt others, will you teach me that too?

ORNIFLE

A useless accomplishment. Other people are simply begging to get hurt. Why complicate one's own life and deprive them of that pleasure? Have some more foie gras. You aren't eating a thing.

FABRICE

(*Pulling a file out of his bag and throwing it at* ORNIFLE.)

There!

ORNIFLE

(*Reading the cover.*)

"Azur Agency, Private Investigations. Divorces." What's this?

FABRICE

(*Shrugging.*)

Your life. Before she died, Mother received a small legacy. I spent what was left on making a thorough investigation of you. I didn't want to run the risk of killing you if you had reformed.

ORNIFLE

And you relied on the Azur Agency to tell you that?

FABRICE

(*Anxiously, like a small boy.*)

Yes. Isn't it a good firm?

ORNIFLE

A fine time to ask! What did it cost you?

FABRICE

Everything.

ORNIFLE

How do you mean, everything?

FABRICE

One hundred and fifty thousand francs.

ORNIFLE

(*Abruptly.*)

Does Marguerite like jewelry?

FABRICE

(*Disconcerted.*)

Yes. Why?

ORNIFLE

(*Turning on him.*)

Don't you think you would have done better to buy Marguerite a ring instead of flinging several hundred thousand francs down the drain, just so that some mangy flatfoot could confirm that your father was a swine? All you had to do was come to me. I'd have told you myself, for nothing. I hate to see money thrown away.

FABRICE

Honor demanded that I know the exact truth.

ORNIFLE

One can never know the exact truth about anything, my poor boy. There's another thing I'll have to teach you.

FABRICE

Anyway, your whole life is in that file. Shall we take a look? Even dipping into it, you'll see, isn't very pretty. It's one long chain of infamy!

ORNIFLE

(*Conciliatory.*)

You pay too much attention to details. You must see the picture as a whole.

FABRICE

And so we will! When you left for Greece, after deserting my mother, it wasn't on a business trip, as you had told her. That's lie number one. There will be others.

ORNIFLE

(*Sighing.*)

I'm afraid there will. But you know, a lie is sometimes a rudimentary form of truth.

94

FABRICE

No! A lie is a lie!

ORNIFLE

(*Regretfully.*)

You're too young to understand. I see that I am going to have to die of remorse. Go on.

FABRICE

You weren't alone in Athens. You stayed at the Acropolis Hotel with a certain Lucette Percivale.

ORNIFLE

(*Delightedly, as he eats and drinks.*)

Tall, fair, stupid, with admirable thighs. Did they put that in the report?

FABRICE

Twenty-five years later that detail does not seem to have impressed itself on the memory of the hall porter.

ORNIFLE

The fellow must go about with his eyes shut. That was the only thing about her worth remembering. I did, in point of fact, take the Orient Express with a pair of thighs, a pair of handsome thighs saddled with a dim young blonde. You may say I could have taken those thighs less far afield—Deauville, for instance, would have met the case quite well. But I was very young. I did things in the grand manner.

FABRICE

Two weeks later you put the young woman back on the train, having made the acquaintance of the daughter of a Belgian Embassy clerk, who comes to visit you for some time at your hotel.

ORNIFLE

(*Dismissing her.*)

Another featherbrain. I'd forgotten her. One does, you know.

FABRICE

(*Continuing his report.*)

Until the day when, having taken up with a local girl who kept an oyster bar, you set up house together in a small room in the Piraeus, where one loses track of you. You reappear, shortly after, at the International Hospital, with a knife wound in the ribs.

ORNIFLE

The oyster girl had another friend called Sophocles—like the real one, except that our boy took love seriously. I don't know if you've noticed, but there isn't a single love scene in the whole of the Greek drama. They were folk with some sense of decency. Who's next?

FABRICE

(*Outraged, throwing down the file.*)

You are unspeakable!

ORNIFLE

(*Astonished.*)

Why?

FABRICE

I had hoped that this record of your doings would make you feel ashamed.

ORNIFLE

Ashamed of what? I'm quite prepared to feel ashamed, I'm firmly resolved to be ashamed, I do sincerely feel the time has come; but I must know exactly what I'm to feel ashamed about.

FABRICE

I had hoped that the vanity of what you term a life of pleasure would at least seem clear to you! My mother loved you! Out of those stray ends of life she could have woven a deep and lasting love!

ORNIFLE

(*Gently.*)

If I had loved your mother, do you think I should have left? Love is a gift from God. I can only speak from hearsay, but I know that it isn't something one refuses. But I didn't love your mother. . . . You have spent a lot of money to discover that a little late. If I had married her and we had brought you up together, you would have learned it rather sooner, and it would have cost you even more. Innocent little recruit in this unequal combat . . . would you have been any happier? I wonder. There's a lot to be said for being an orphan.

FABRICE

(*Stands nonplused for a second, then bursts out.*)

You're a monster!

ORNIFLE

(*Suddenly weary.*)

No, no. That's a much-abused word. Is it my fault if we're living on the moon? You remember, in Jules Verne you lift a finger, thinking to say hello to somebody, and pfft! you're already miles away. The experience of happiness is a terrifying thing. It teaches one that life has no weight.

(*Suddenly.*)

Do you love Marguerite?

FABRICE

With all my heart and for always.

ORNIFLE

And do you never feel the urge to cry out with longing sometimes in the street, when another girl goes by? A girl who'll never be yours—since you already love another.

FABRICE

No, never.

ORNIFLE

(*Smiling a rather grim smile and patting his shoulder.*)

Then you don't know your luck. You've been spared a dog's life. You have your seat already booked in heaven and you can claim the esteem of your fellow men by way of bonus.

(*Listening at the window.*)

I hear the enormous door of Machetu's enormous car. He'll be here in a second, and fifteen minutes later your old wizard of a father will have won your sweetheart back for you. Only, you have a lifetime ahead of you in which to lose her. Take care not to bore her. That's the one thing they never can forgive us for.

FABRICE

I won't care if I bore her!

ORNIFLE

I'm sure you won't, my little man. But she will.

97

ACT FOUR

(ORNIFLE's *bedroom.*

MACHETU *comes in with* MARGUERITE. *She is very young and very lovely, and it will be impossible not to feel that* ORNIFLE *is aware of it.*)

MACHETU

Your Grace, here is the young lady you ordered. But it's not Pilu's consent you want. It's hers. She refuses to have anything more to do with your son.

FABRICE

(*Seizing her by the wrist.*)

Why didn't you wait for me?

MARGUERITE

(*Equally aggressively.*)

Why did you go in? I told you! I said, "If you go in, then you can't love me and I'll never speak to you again." I shouted it at you through the window as you were ringing the bell. You pretended not to hear. Then I opened the car door wide and I put one foot on the pavement. You can't say I didn't give you fair warning. You must have seen me—you turned around.

FABRICE

I thought you were just pretending to get out.

MARGUERITE

And I thought you were pretending to go in! But the door opened and in you went. I thought you must be waiting just inside, to give me a fright. I counted up to a hundred and fifty.

FABRICE

(*Bitterly.*)

A hundred and fifty. That's your love. . . . A girl who really cared wouldn't have counted at all.

MARGUERITE

(*Tears springing to her eyes.*)

I counted all the way up to a hundred and fifty twice, if you want to know—very slowly. But when I saw that you definitely weren't coming out again, I wrote you that letter and I left—all alone, through the deserted streets, in the pitch dark! A man followed me!

FABRICE

(*Leaping up.*)

What did he want?

MARGUERITE

Ten francs. He'd just come out of the hospital and all his children were dying. I hadn't a penny on me. I had to walk all the way home. And my new shoes were hurting me. I told you when we bought them this afternoon they were too small! But you always have to be right! How can you love a man who always wants to be right!

FABRICE

(*Frantic.*)

Marguerite——

MARGUERITE

(*Tragically.*)

When the pain got too bad, I took them off. And I went on, barefoot. My stockings are ruined. My feet are cut and bleeding——

FABRICE

(*Utterly lost.*)

Marguerite . . . foot injuries can be very dangerous. . . . I've some Mercurochrome in my bag——

MARGUERITE

(*Stepping back.*)

Don't touch me! I'll never let you touch me again! Your patricide's hands make me shudder——

FABRICE

(*Groaning.*)

But I didn't kill him!

MARGUERITE

(*Shrugging.*)

I know that. I took the bullets out of the gun. But you chose to do it and run the risk of losing me. It was between him and me, and you chose him! I'll never forgive you for that. This time tomorrow I'll be on the plane, all alone, brokenhearted. . . . I'll try to sleep, but sleep won't come. Anyway, the plane will probably crash——

FABRICE

(*Wringing his hands in anguish.*)

Marguerite——

MARGUERITE

(*Already far away.*)

The others will be screaming in terror. Not I. After all I've suffered, it will be a blessed release. . . . I shall smile and astonish them all by my composure. Unfortunately, there will be no survivors, so no one will be able to come to you and say: As the aircraft dived into the murky waters, she was smiling. I hope that vision haunts you for the rest of your days! Anyway, survivors or no survivors, I'll have you know that I died smiling. I'm telling you so in advance.

FABRICE

(*In tears.*)

Marguerite——

(MARGUERITE *goes out majestically.*

Yelling as he darts after her.)
Marguerite!

ORNIFLE

(*Restraining him.*)
Don't worry. That's the bathroom. She'll be back.

MACHETU

(*With a lump in his throat.*)
Aren't they sweet?

ORNIFLE

Aren't they silly! That's love for you.

(MARGUERITE *reappears, still dignified, despite her mistake.*)

MARGUERITE

Excuse me. That was the bathroom. Which is the way out, please?

ORNIFLE

I'll show you. But first I should like to talk to you a minute. May I?

MARGUERITE

(*Giving him an appraising look.*)
I gather from Fabrice, who gave me his little report to read, that you make a specialty of how to talk to girls. But if you think you can talk me around, I advise you to think again. Words can't mend a broken heart.

ORNIFLE

(*Sympathetically.*)
Alas, how well I know it!

(*Pouring out champagne.*)
A glass of champagne won't hurt, though, will it, after all this excitement? I swear I shan't preach at you. I wouldn't know how. I merely think it's a pity, just because my son chooses to make an idiot of himself, that I should forfeit the pleasure of meeting a young lady who is still ravishing, despite her broken heart.

MARGUERITE

(*Hostile.*)
You're out of date. We've had one, if not two, wars since compliments made any impression on a girl.

ORNIFLE

(*Ruefully.*)

I have met my match, I see. Machetu, take Fabrice next door and show him my paintings. I'm sure that two minds of your caliber will have some fascinating views on modern art.

(*He shepherds them out and comes back to* MARGUERITE.)

MARGUERITE

That's another of your delusions. Fabrice doesn't know the first thing about art.

ORNIFLE

Nor does Machetu. That is why their discussion is bound to be enthralling. There are artless artists whose canvases fetch thousands. Why should the opinion of artless connoisseurs not have its value too?

MARGUERITE

(*Consents to laugh a little.*)

Do you know, when we went to the Louvre, what he made me look at? "The Rape of the Sabines."

ORNIFLE

Is he interested in rape?

MARGUERITE

No. In the Romans. Fabrice idolized the Romans at school. It's poisoned his whole system.

ORNIFLE

(*Delighted, handing her a glass.*)

So there are minds, then, underneath those ponytails?

MARGUERITE

Is this the first time you've realized it?

ORNIFLE

At my age a man tends to frequent women who have their hair done twice a week. A young girl is Greek to me. Do go on. You fascinate me.

MARGUERITE

I thought you wanted to talk to me?

ORNIFLE

(*Smiling.*)

Yes, but I see that I have so many things to learn. I think I'll listen to you instead.

MARGUERITE

That won't be difficult. I never stop talking. Fabrice hates it. He says that if you talk all the time, you never have a chance to think. I say it's the reverse. When I'm not talking, I haven't a thought in my head. But the moment I open my mouth, I start to think of something. That's a common subject for a quarrel. On our good days, that is. Because that one never goes very far.

ORNIFLE

Do you quarrel about a lot of things?

MARGUERITE

We counted up to a hundred and two. The permanent ones. That's not counting casual quarrels. Those can flare up over anything at all.

ORNIFLE

(*Seriously.*)

Life must be hell for you!

MARGUERITE

(*Sighing.*)

Yes, it is. That's why I think it's better if I end it all.

ORNIFLE

Suppose the plane doesn't crash—just for the sake of argument, of course. How long do you give yourself in South Africa to forget Fabrice?

MARGUERITE

(*Sincerely.*)

But it never occurred to me that the plane might not crash!

ORNIFLE

I know, but say it doesn't—these things happen. You sue the company and you get your money back. What then?

MARGUERITE

(*On the verge of tears.*)

That's right, laugh at me! Do you think it's easy, being a girl?

ORNIFLE

(*Moved.*)

No, my poor little dove. It's the hardest thing in the world. Have you read the history of the Caesars?

MARGUERITE

No. I haven't read anything. I passed my first exam because I smiled at the boy at the next desk and he slipped me all his cribs. And I passed my oral because I made the examiner blush so much, he didn't know what he was doing. So he answered his own questions and gave himself an A minus for my worst subject. But I'm a dunce. I don't know anything. That's another reason why Fabrice can't love me. He knows everything.

ORNIFLE

Well, now, you'll learn, if you read Suetonius, or even if you don't, that it is just that combination of weakness and excessive power which makes the lives of Roman emperors and pretty girls so difficult. A boy has to slave his insides out before grown men, clinging like grim death to their office desks, will concede that he shows promise. A chit of a girl, who only yesterday was playing hopscotch, has only to put her hair up and walk in, and immediately they'll sit up and take notice.

MARGUERITE

Do you think that isn't depressing for a girl?

ORNIFLE

What?

MARGUERITE

The fuss men make over you. That's why I fell in love with Fabrice. My little girlish wiles had no effect on him.

(*Exclaiming in a flash of temper.*)

But he's much too much of a bore.

ORNIFLE

> Young man Gaiety
> Longed to join the dance,

> Young man Duty
> Gave it ne'er a glance.

MARGUERITE

(*Looking up at him with amused interest.*)
How pretty! Is it yours? Fabrice told me that you used to write very lovely poems, once.

ORNIFLE

Funny. Everybody thinks it's mine. Unfortunately it's by Péguy.

MARGUERITE

(*None the wiser.*)
Péguy?

ORNIFLE

Yes. I see that I could safely have told you it was mine.
(*Sighing.*)
However, two hours ago I decided to be honest. I must try to keep it up a little longer.

> Young man Gaiety
> Longed to join the dance,
> Young man Duty
> Gave it ne'er a glance.

Do you know what it means?

MARGUERITE

(*Smiling.*)
I do believe you're going to explain the text and give me an A minus, like the examiner. I can't get over it!

ORNIFLE

You won't get over it until you're old—for you will grow old too, you know. . . . Until then you must resign yourself to getting good marks which you don't deserve. But that doesn't absolve you from having to choose. Young man Duty. And young man Gaiety. There are two of them, and unfortunately they are never the same one. You have to choose.

(MARGUERITE *does not answer.*)
What made you love Fabrice?

MARGUERITE

(*Quietly, after a short hesitation.*)

He was poor. He despised money. . . . And at home, with Daddy, ever since I was a little girl, I'd heard so much talk about money, that I thought that was wonderful. He was sad too. . . . Papa has an ulcer because he never knows whether he'll make another million or land in jail again, but my brothers and my mother are always so gay! Mama is brimming with youth since she started growing old. So Fabrice's gravity, even his dullness, seemed such a gay adventure! We were going to run away together and be poor and live the serious life. I was going to sweep his house and wash his dishes. Each time I fancied a new dress, we would buy him a textbook—and you need a good many, you know, when you study medicine! Every time I felt like going out, he would study a new chapter and I would type his notes for him. Then, when he qualified, he would go and look after aborigines in equatorial Africa. That seemed so distinguished beside the gilded cage that I was meant for. Only . . .

ORNIFLE

(*Gently.*)

Only?

MARGUERITE

Fabrice annoyed me a little more than usual this evening, with that honor of his—and now I'm wondering whether I'm not a gilded bird like all the others and whether I wouldn't do better to fly back into the cage. . . . It can be fun, after all, to be given A minus for nothing. It can be fun, too, being happy and doing all the silly things you feel like doing when you feel like doing them, like a little gadfly.

(*Winsomely.*)

Do you know that feeling, you who know it all?

ORNIFLE

(*Watching her, in panic, transform herself into a cat.*)

Help me, ye shades of Galahad!

MARGUERITE

(*Wide-eyed.*)

What's the matter? Who are you calling?

ORNIFLE

A strong man I know.
(MACHETU *appears.*)

MACHETU

Did you call?

ORNIFLE

Machetu! Saved! No, Fabrice, you come back later. Only Machetu.
(*He closes the door.*)
You stand over there. Don't move. Don't say anything. But stay put.
I need a witness.

MACHETU

(*Ironically.*)
Having a duel?

ORNIFLE

Yes.

(*Going to* MARGUERITE.)
My dear . . . my child . . . there is something very penetrating in
what you have just said, but it's completely wrong! I'll tell you the real
truth of it. There is only one reality, one thing that satisfies hunger
and can be eaten like an honest crust of bread, and that is love. The
rest is candyfloss, chocolate fondants, nausea. You pounce on the
box; you take another, and another, and then one more, swearing
it will be the last. But it never is the last. And at the end of the
afternoon you're sitting by the empty box and wishing you were
dead. And you've nothing left but a bit of soiled cardboard and a
few scraps of paper sticking to your fingers.

MARGUERITE

(*Moaning.*)
But think of the good things of life slipping away!

ORNIFLE

The more they slip, the better it will be. Your love must cost you a
hundred dresses and a thousand little pleasures. Your love must cost
you very, very dear—and the more it fleeces you, the richer you will
be. It's the first step that costs so much, Marguerite, my little flower;

the first penny is the only real expense. After that, when you start giving, you'll see how easy it will be. There'll be no stopping you. It's the first little pleasure standing in love's way that you'll find difficult. It is at the first party to which you do not go—so as not to dance with some other young man—that love awaits you.

MARGUERITE

Did you ever take that step?

ORNIFLE

No, never. That's why you must believe me. I am dying of it. Ask Machetu.

MACHETU

(*Pierced by this.*)

Oi-oi-oi.

ORNIFLE

Machetu says, "Oi-oi-oi." That's the sure sign, in him of a profound and subtle observation. I flounder in rhetoric. But Machetu says, "Oi-oi-oi." That ought to convince you. Oi-oi-oi, my little Marguerite, oi-oi-oi, if you only knew!

MACHETU

(*The echo.*)

Oi-oi-oi.

ORNIFLE

(*Curtly.*)

All right. You've made your point.

(*Going to* MARGUERITE *and taking her hands.*)

Marguerite, this may surprise you, but there's a soul under that little ponytail, just as there was beneath Isolde's heavy golden braids, and it is the same one. And all the objects in the world won't give it a single crust of bread. It needs another soul to snuggle up to, to make the trip with, side by side like oxen. And when one of the oxen is sick, the other is sick too. When one ox dies in harness, the other ox won't plow and they have to send it to the butcher.

(MACHETU *sniffles.*)
No comments, Machetu!

MACHETU
(*Swallowing his tears.*)
All right.

ORNIFLE
Look, Marguerite, there's that old louse Machetu in tears, yet all I've done is preach you a bad sermon. Be Fabrice's ox. Bend to the yoke together. Twenty's the age for seriousness. After that it can't be done. You must give while you're still rich. Time enough to act the goat when you're your mother's age.

MARGUERITE
(*Softly, half won over.*)
We'll bicker all the time.

ORNIFLE
It will be bliss.

MARGUERITE
(*Looking up at him.*)
But suppose I begin to be bored?

ORNIFLE
(*A trifle recklessly.*)
You'll come and tell me so.
(*Pushing her.*)
Go and fetch Fabrice. He's probably standing in front of my Picassos thinking what a weird shape the world must be. And come back in here to kiss and make up. I want to see you do it.

MARGUERITE
(*Looking at him with a little wondering smile.*)
It's funny. I don't know why, but you're the one I can confide in, not him.
(*She goes out.*)

ORNIFLE
(*Striding over to* MACHETU *and seizing his arm.*)
Machetu, don't leave me!

MACHETU
(*His voice hoarse with emotion.*)
But . . . did **you** believe all those things you were telling her?

ORNIFLE
(*Sincerely.*)
Almost, at the time. What an evening! Anyway, I promised him I'd get her back. Phew! That's done. I've been a father to him. Lord, it's exhausting!

(MARGUERITE *storms back in again, followed by* FABRICE, *stiffer and more unyielding than ever.*)

MARGUERITE
This is the limit! Now *he* won't have *me!*

FABRICE
After what has occurred, my mind is made up. I was given to understand that Marguerite was not in love with me.

ORNIFLE
(*Bearing down on them, roaring with rage.*)
Oh, no you don't! I've had enough. I'm not singing a hymn to true love twice in one evening! You're at the silly age, I know, but don't overdo it. Marguerite loves you, you idiot. She went to fetch you, didn't she? She's willing to pay for your love with all the little pleasures you'll never have the wit to give her. Then pay for hers with a bit of that stiff neck of yours, you cussed young mule! There's another way of letting true love pass you by and that's by spelling it with a capital *L*. I know your love isn't perfect yet, but you've a lifetime ahead of you to work on it. It'll give you something to do on Sundays! Look at her; there are tears in her eyes, you ruffian! And in yours too, come to that. Kiss each other, will you!

(*He pushes them into each other's arms.* FABRICE *and* MARGUERITE *look at each other through their tears, then they smile, and slowly their arms wind round each other. With a deep sigh they hold each other close and kiss. Seconds pass.* ORNIFLE *grows visibly unmanned under the strain. Suddenly, unable to stand it a moment longer, he yells.*)

Stop it!

(*The two young people draw apart slightly, in astonishment.*)

FABRICE

Why, what's the matter?

ORNIFLE

When you've finished! Mauling each other in that indecent fashion before a dying man!

FABRICE

Are you mad?

ORNIFLE

(*Beside himself.*)

By my deathbed! Like rabbits! I blush for you.

(*Brutally, going to* FABRICE.)

How dare you be my son and twenty years of age and in my shoes! You thief!

(*He looks at them, distorted with jealousy, and shouts.*)

Can't you even wait until I'm cold?

FABRICE

But look here, this is absurd. You aren't dead yet!

ORNIFLE

Yes, I am! I took God at his word! The spell is broken. You said too much a while ago. Life isn't funny any more. Death has frozen it in imbecilic attitudes, like a bad film that snapped. While the thing moved, the illusion held. But motionless, with fist clenched for the punch that never follows through, lips parted for the kiss that never comes, the hand forever on the heart and nothing in the eyes—we are grotesque! So that's your precious love? I can just see it in two years from now! Pouah! So that's all living was! And there's death to be got through into the bargain! They should have warned me. I wouldn't have troubled to be born!

MARGUERITE

(*Crying out in alarm.*)

Why, what's the matter with you? You look quite pale!

(FABRICE *grasps his bag.*)

FABRICE

Lie down! I'll give you an injection.

ORNIFLE

(*Shakes him off and says dully.*)

No. There's no injection can cure that, you fool. I am jealous.

(*There is a frightened silence.* MLLE. SUPO *enters.*)

MLLE. SUPO

Father Dubaton is here.

ORNIFLE

(*Turning on her.*)

Who gave him the bright idea of calling at this hour? It was you, wasn't it, you wretched girl?

MLLE. SUPO

(*Stammering.*)

Dr. Subites doesn't seem to want to bother, and I couldn't find Madame, so I thought——

ORNIFLE

Never think! You haven't the brains for it.

(*To the others.*)

Go into my sitting room, you two. Have a rest or kiss each other if you must—out of my sight. I'll call you.

(*To* FABRICE.)

You're not to leave this house until my own doctor arrives. Is that clear? Machetu, show the way.

(*The others go out.* ORNIFLE *goes to meet* FR. DUBATON.)

I am distressed at Supo's zeal, Father. Heaven preserve us from zeal. Had you not gone to bed?

FR. DUBATON

I was already up, my son. I was praying. The end of term is always such a busy time that we only have the nights in which to pay a little attention to Our Lord.

ORNIFLE

I wouldn't want that idiot girl to have dragged you out in the middle of the night for nothing. I owe you a dying man, Father. You shall have one. We'll play our scene at last, after the times we've put it off. Would you like it in the form of a confession?

FR. DUBATON

A little chat or a confession—whichever you prefer, my son.

ORNIFLE

(*Bringing up a chair.*)

Confession, then. It's more straightforward. Will an ordinary chair do? (ORNIFLE *kneels down before* FR. DUBATON.)

Forgive me, Father, for I have sinned too little!

FR. DUBATON

(*Gently.*)

Do not mock, my son. You have led me to expect nothing but candor from you. What do you mean, exactly?

ORNIFLE

I mean that only the sins we have committed can be shriven. The others putrify eternally. I repent of all the sins I never had the courage to commit, Father—the foulest, the ones you'll not be able to wash clean. I have had one on my conscience for the last five minutes that stinks to heaven already.

(*He gets to his feet.*)

You work among souls; you must see some fine ones, with the righteous. All those ingrowing lusts . . . that must give off a high old stench!

FR. DUBATON

(*With a slight smile.*)

It doesn't always smell too sweet. But our noses grow inured, after a while, in our little boxes, to the smell of men. And sometimes, from the worst of sinners, there wafts, through the grille, a scent as of wisteria and honeysuckle in a summer garden.

ORNIFLE

From a sinner, maybe. But what about your bigoted old maids, with nothing to confess but a cross word to their cat; do they ever smell good?

FR. DUBATON

(*With a smile.*)

Never. But let us not beat a dead horse, my son. We've better things to do. You know as well as I do that we can't stand the bigoted old besoms either.

(*With a comic little sigh.*)

Those are *our* better halves!

ORNIFLE

There is an element of caricature about them which embarrasses you. But do you care for folk who never sin at all?

FR. DUBATON

(*Lightly.*)

Of course not. They take the bread out of our mouths.

ORNIFLE

(*Moving away, testily.*)

I'm no match for you. I see your little game. You've made up your mind to win me over, willy-nilly, *in extremis.*

(*With sudden fury.*)

Take care, Father! The Church is too ready these days with its kind words and coaxing hands. A priest is a priest. It's not for him to handle sinners with kid gloves. His job is to make a nuisance of himself with his black skirts and his empty pockets and his chastity. I am a no-good swine, we know, but I warn you here and now, you won't catch me by making allowances for me. I have a horror of facile excuses. This sounds odd coming from me, but five times out of ten, I only sinned under duress.

FR. DUBATON

Duress, my son?

ORNIFLE

Duress, Father! It's no joke, living for pleasure. Many's the time I would sooner have curled up with a good book. But I said to myself, No. You wanted her, my lad, and you shall have her. You'll say all the right things, you'll tell her that you love her, even if it makes you retch. If she plays hard to get, you'll badger her at her front door, dizzy with fatigue, until she lets you in. You'll go through all the motions one by one and look as though you like it. Until the moment when, the pleasure given and received, you find yourself alone beside this unknown meat, wondering what in Satan's name you're doing there. That's what's meant by sin, Father. No need for Divine book-keeping there; it's paid for C.O.D.

FR. DUBATON

My poor son.

ORNIFLE

Keep your sympathy. There's nothing I hate more. I should have despised myself ten times more if, having wanted a girl, I hadn't done my damnedest to get her, knowing full well what was in store for me.

(*Abruptly.*)

Do you know how my father died?

FR. DUBATON

No.

ORNIFLE

He died at the wheel of his Dion-Bouton, flattened against a tree trunk at fifty miles an hour—that was a lot in those days—through having looked one second too long at the haunches of a farm girl pulling carrots in a field. The woman ran to help the plowboys who were laying him beside the ditch, and before he breathed his last, my father had the time to notice that he had died for a toothless old girl of seventy. Funny, don't you think? Go on, laugh. I laughed when his valet, who survived, told me the story afterwards. Yet I was fond of my father. God, when He gave men desire, might have given them a little more discrimination while He was about it. It's not quite foolproof, that little invention of His.

FR. DUBATON

He wanted all things to be difficult and true love to be rare.

ORNIFLE

He needn't have worried. It is rare. But need He have been quite so lavish with the illusion—and the anguish that He gave to some, of not being able to have everything? I call that most unreasonable of Him.

FR. DUBATON

(*Gently.*)

But God isn't reasonable! Whatever gave you that idea?

(*A pause.*)

Is there anything I can do for you, my son? I know you expect scant help from my ministrations, and I don't want to lay absolution over you like a blanket. What can I do for you?

ORNIFLE

(*Kindly.*)

Nothing, Father. And believe me, I'm sorry. I wish you could.

FR. DUBATON

(*In a murmur.*)

It's chiefly for me that it's sad. It's my vestments that bother you. A man who loves another can always do something for him.

(*He gets up.*)

You see, I think we began our scene on the wrong foot. The tempo was too dramatic at the start. Where have all those high phrases got us? In the old days we had a good laugh together, you and I. And very nice it was. Tonight you've wrapped yourself in a positive pall of satanic gloom because that young man told you that you weren't too well. You know, medicine is a very splendid thing, but when all's said and done, God still has the final say. You'll probably bury us both. One word before I go. Beneath all your bravado—forgive the word, I'm talking to you as an older man now, not a priest—I feel a kind of reticence, which prevents you from being frank with me. We aren't sweet sixteen you know, despite our robes. We are humanity's garbage men, and in the long run we know more than the most hardened libertines. So come along, put your cards on the table, there's a good fellow. Between ourselves, why so many women?

ORNIFLE

(*Murmuring.*)

It was the only thing that amused me.

FR. DUBATON

Did you never fall in love, then?

ORNIFLE

Yes, once. With my wife, as a matter of fact, but . . .

FR. DUBATON

But . . . ?

ORNIFLE

(*Kindly.*)

That's not a tale for your ears, Father.

FR. DUBATON

I don't know anything about it, I realize that. But when I visit my brother in the Rhone valley, during the holidays, we go to eat in a little fisherman's bistro where I'm very partial to the wine. I ask for the same one, year after year. When you're really fond of something, it seems to me that the only sensible thing is to come back for more. And when you've found the nice little red wine that suits you, you stick to it. For a while, anyway.

ORNIFLE

(*Smiles and says kindly, after a short pause.*)

The analogy isn't quite accurate, Father. The taste of wine improves with keeping. The taste of love grows sour.

FR. DUBATON

In other words, what really amused you was uncorking different bottles and taking a sip or two from each?

(*With a hint of mischief.*)

I'm going to tell you something—even if you do think I'm a tippler. You don't really love good wine.

ORNIFLE

(*With a grave smile.*)

You may be right. I hadn't thought of that.

(*Enter* NENETTE.)

NENETTE

The doctors have arrived, sir.

FR. DUBATON

I'll leave you in other hands. Nowadays, one jokes with priests, but never with physicians. Don't bother to see me to the door. Like all traveling salesmen, I know the way out.

(*He goes.* ORNIFLE *remains, lost in thought, in the middle of the stage. Then he shakes himself and murmurs.*)

ORNIFLE

The old illusionist! My brother showman. Another minute and my head was in the bag.

(*He muses a while longer.*)

Well, well, well . . . Nenette!

NENETTE

Sir?

ORNIFLE

Go to the florists and tell them to send along all the best roses in the shop.

NENETTE

Here?

ORNIFLE

Yes. For Madame.

(*He goes over to her, his old self again.*)

Did you show those two buffoons into the study? Give me a hand with the rest of this stuff. I've got to the stage when I don't know what I can do and what I can't. For all I know, I might be committing suicide by taking off my shoes. It's stupid enough having to die. They might at least devise a way of doing it in comfort.

NENETTE

(*Helping him out of his costume.*)

Mlle. Marie Pêche telephoned earlier this evening to say she could see you whenever you were free. She will be ringing again first thing in the morning, before she goes to the studio. What am I to say to her?

ORNIFLE

(*Dreams a little, then gives a harassed sigh.*)

Tell her that I'm rather busy just now.

(*He goes toward the bathroom, while* NENETTE *trots after him, unhooking him.*)

Do you think you have a soul, Nenette?

NENETTE

(*Unruffled.*)

Everybody has a soul. Is this the first time you've given the matter any thought, sir?

ORNIFLE

Yes. For the first time, today. And I wish you wouldn't call me "sir." We aren't in company now.

(*He turns her round suddenly.*)

Look at me.

NENETTE

(*Averting her face in embarrassment.*)

No. I don't care to be looked at any more.

ORNIFLE

(*Smiling.*)

Since when?

NENETTE

Around the time when you stopped wanting to look at me.

ORNIFLE

(*With sudden affection.*)

What a pretty thing you were, Nenette!

NENETTE

(*Quietly, without rancor.*)

For a bit of fun——

ORNIFLE

(*With comic indignation.*)

Oh, how tedious you all are, with those souls of yours!

(*He slaps her gaily on the bottom.*)

Come on! Come and help me!

NENETTE

(*Sighing as she follows him out.*)

The heart's not in it any more.

ORNIFLE

(*With a touch of asperity as he goes into the bathroom.*)

The heart's not what it was!

ACT FIVE

(ORNIFLE's *bedroom.*

MLLE. SUPO *and* MACHETU *appear to be waiting.* MACHETU *is pacing up and down.*)

MACHETU

They're taking their time listening to his heart! Is that a good sign or a bad sign?

MLLE. SUPO

May be good, may be bad. It depends.

MACHETU

(*After a pause.*)

Was it he who told you to call me at Mlle. Mercadier's?

MLLE. SUPO

(*Shrugging.*)

He was unconscious.

MACHETU

Then how did you know I was there?

MLLE. SUPO

(*Shortly.*)

I know everything.

MACHETU

Then try to know a bit less in future, do you mind?

MLLE. SUPO

(*Contemptuous.*)

I am not even listening to you.

MACHETU

What are you doing, then?

MLLE. SUPO

I am giving thanks.

MACHETU

(*Goggling at her.*)

This is a madhouse! It's all one big riddle. Here's a joker spends the whole of last evening persuading me that his girl is in love with me, when I never even mentioned her. I take his advice and I force myself on her in spite of an icy reception. I sweat blood getting her to stop crying and sit down to supper with me. Luckily, I spilled a glass onto the tablecloth and said a word I shouldn't, and that made her giggle. Right, so after the chicken, the atmosphere seems to be easing up a bit; we're about to tackle the rum baba when you ring up to say the Maestro's sinking fast. I drop everything. I dash over and I find him in the best of health, talking away nineteen to the dozen about things I can't make head nor tail of. What is all this about a chattel? I never heard anything so daft.

MLLE. SUPO

It was inspired! But you didn't understand a word of it, naturally.

MACHETU

The priest arrived just as I was seeing daylight. So then I lost the thread. Anyway, I'm tired of being a laughingstock. I'm an easygoing fellow, but enough is enough. He should have asked me before he gave me the key, whether I had a soul or not!

MLLE. SUPO

How could someone like you understand anything about the miracle you saw tonight! That terrible attack was heaven sent. I know now that the Maestro can be saved.

MACHETU

Saved from what?

MLLE. SUPO

From himself! The day I have been waiting for so long has come at last; I feel it! I see, as it were, a spiritual dawn arise!

MACHETU

(*Looking at his watch.*)

I don't know about spiritual, but it's dawn all right. And I'd like to know if I can go back now. Women are like soup—you mustn't let them get cold.

MLLE. SUPO

(*With a mirthless laugh.*)

Like soup! How could the Maestro endure a vulgar creature like you for so long? Run back to your little strumpet, do! What difference can it possibly make to us, now?

MACHETU

(*Pathetically.*)

I can't. He took back the key.

(*The door opens. Enter the two* DOCTORS, *still in fancy dress, and* ORNIFLE. *They are in high spirits and smoking enormous cigars.*)

GALOPIN

(*With righteous rage.*)

My dear fellow, I absolutely insist on knowing the name of that young jackanapes! In his third year, you say? I'm on the Board of Examiners. Just wait till he comes up before me. I'll settle his hash, make no mistake about that! Bishop's disease! Ignoramus!

SUBITES

(*Equally outraged.*)

Bishop's disease—and no syncope! Numbskull!

GALOPIN

With not a trace of tachycardia! Mountebank!

SUBITES

Perfect mitral frequency! No diastole!

GALOPIN

A pulse of eighty! Percussion absolutely normal! I'll pin his ears back!

SUBITES

No hypertension! I'll knock his silly head off! Go and fetch him. I can't wait to confound the little moron!

GALOPIN

We can have the law on him, you realize that? Illegal practice of medicine! What right had he to go listening to your heart? What right had he to give you an injection?

ORNIFLE

I had passed out.

GALOPIN

I can't help that! He should have left you unconscious until the arrival of a qualified practitioner. That is a cardinal rule in medicine. Otherwise, any hamfisted meddler can kill our patient before we do. Fetch him here this instant! I've smelled blood! If I don't dress him down this instant, I'm the one who'll have an attack. A real one this time. My heart is ten times weaker than yours is, my dear fellow.

ORNIFLE

I'll get him.

(*He goes.*)

GALOPIN

(*To* SUBITES.)

Nice Picasso he has out there. Poor period though. A good thing I didn't listen to you. I couldn't have borne to leave the ball before the end. Delightful evening! The women were ravishing. The fashion suits them very well this winter. By the way, I heard a first-class joke this evening. Do you know the one about the hedgehog who forgot his toothbrush?

SUBITES

(*More sycophantic than ever.*)

No, my dear Professor. I can't wait to hear it. You do tell them so well!

123

GALOPIN

It's quite good, this one. A hedgehog goes on his honeymoon——
(*He turns and sees* ORNIFLE, *who is still on the threshold.*)
Still here?

ORNIFLE

Yes. I've changed my mind. I won't fetch him.

GALOPIN

Why not?

ORNIFLE

It's too cruel.

GALOPIN

You can never be too cruel with cretins! Suppose you really were a
heart case. That lad could have killed you with his faulty diagnosis.

ORNIFLE

If, on the other hand, I did have a weak heart, his diagnosis would
have been correct. However, as I haven't, I would rather let him
think that he was right. He's only in his third year. He'll improve.

SUBITES

Wait till he gets a practice. What a bloodbath!

ORNIFLE

I don't care if he kills other people. I won't consult him, anyway.

GALOPIN

You must be mad! Or a saint. Same thing. I wish I knew the young
scamp's name, though. I should have liked to cook his goose for him
at the exams. However, please yourself.
(*To* SUBITES.)
Come along, my dear chap. I have to be at the hospital in half an
hour. And if I appear in this getup, I don't think the staff would
take me seriously. These days it's the over-all that makes the man.

ORNIFLE

I'll see you out. I can't thank you enough, Doctor. I have spent an
agonizing night. Thanks to you, the nightmare is over.

SUBITES

(*Following them.*)

If you had come to the ball, you'd have saved yourself all the bother of a death agony. Let that be a lesson to you. Always listen to your medical adviser, even in matters of medicine.

(*He follows them out.*)

GALOPIN

(*Off.*)

Yes, a hedgehog went on his honeymoon without his toothbrush. . . .

MLLE. SUPO

(*Clasping her hands together.*)

Thank you, God! If he had died, I was as good as dead! But save him completely, Lord!

MACHETU

Aren't you ever satisfied?

MLLE. SUPO

There is still his soul——

MACHETU

(*Exasperated.*)

Soul! It's a positive obsession in this house!

(ORNIFLE *returns.* MACHETU *runs to meet him with open arms, happy as a big fat sheepdog.*

Flinging his arms around him.)

Ah, you old skunk, you! What do you mean by scaring us out of our wits like that? Phew, I haven't got over it yet! I'm fond of you, you old ram—do you know that? Ever since Supo telephoned, I haven't breathed. My only friend! I had visions of you lying dead already. Why, I'd rather have broken both my legs, and that's a fact! Do you need any money?

ORNIFLE

(*Languidly.*)

Naturally. This unexpected recovery alters all my plans. I shall require a great many things. I may travel. . . . After a shock like this,

I need rest. I may ask you for the loan of one of your villas on the Riviera——

MACHETU

When in trouble, send for Machetu. He won't let you down. Come and see me tomorrow in my office.

(*He asks timidly.*)

About the key . . . ?

ORNIFLE

What key?

MACHETU

Melissa's key. What have you decided? You took it back earlier on.

ORNIFLE

(*Vaguely.*)

Did I? I'm sorry, old chap; I'll give it back to you.

(*He looks in his pockets.*)

MACHETU

(*Tentatively.*)

Under your pillow. . . . Do you think that . . . ? After all, if she has a soul, I have one too, haven't I?

ORNIFLE

(*Looking for the key.*)

Yes, of course. . . .

MACHETU

About the "chattel" . . . I must tell you, I couldn't make it out at all. There's a double meaning there that bothers me. If you could spare a minute to explain it quietly, I think I might cotton on to it.

ORNIFLE

(*His thoughts elsewhere.*)

Later. . . . There's no hurry. Here's the key. How were you making out when Supo telephoned?

MACHETU

We were finishing the chicken. We were about to start on the rum baba.

ORNIFLE

(*Severely.*)

Is that all?

MACHETU

(*Shamefaced.*)

It was a fair while before we sat down to supper. You see, she was crying so much . . . I had a lot of trouble comforting her. But things brightened up toward the end. She called me "dear old Roger" once. . . . She even said that I was "different"——

ORNIFLE

(*Pushing him out.*)

It's in the bag. Go straight back and don't waste a minute.

MACHETU

(*Panicking.*)

What if she's asleep? Do I wake her up?

ORNIFLE

A little. Not too much.

MACHETU

(*At the door.*)

And what about the soul . . . ? Do I tell her?

ORNIFLE

(*Bundling him out impatiently.*)

Tell her afterwards! It will give you something to talk about!

(ORNIFLE *has followed* MACHETU *out. When he comes back a second later,* MLLE. SUPO *is standing watching him.*)

What do you think you're staring at?

MLLE. SUPO

I am watching an old man completing his last loathsome gesture.

ORNIFLE

(*Looking at himself in a distant mirror.*)

What old man? I've grown ten years younger since last night!

MLLE. SUPO

(*Smiling.*)

It was a figure of speech. You were right. Neither Machetu nor that little tart were worth your stooping to their level. Let them couple like animals. What does it matter?

ORNIFLE

(*Raising a finger.*)

Pardon me, it matters a great deal. It will prevent some other young idiot from pulling a gun on me in twenty years from now. Are they still in the sitting room?

MLLE. SUPO

Yes. Shall I fetch them? They were still asleep when I looked in just now.

ORNIFLE

I'll go myself. . . . On second thought, no. You go. But only wake the young lady. Tell her I want to talk to her alone.

(MLLE. SUPO *goes out.* ORNIFLE *flings open the window and takes a deep breath. The sun is rising. Outside, the* CHILDREN *from the Institute can be heard singing.*)

CHILDREN

(*Off.*)

> Jesu, you are hiding,
> Jesu, where are you? [etc.]

ORNIFLE

(*In a murmur.*)

I love the early mornings. One hasn't smoked too much . . . or drunk too much. . . . One feels clean all over. And a man can go to perdition with new energy.

(*He combs his hair at the dressing table, sprays himself with perfume, straightens the sheets, and climbs into bed, carefully assuming the pose of an invalid.*

Murmuring.)

The better to eat you with, my child. . . .

(MARGUERITE *comes in, looking lovelier than ever.*)

Marguerite! It does my heart good to see you look so pretty. You give me back my faith in life.

128

MARGUERITE

(*Kindly.*)

Being pretty isn't everything, you know——

ORNIFLE

Who told you that? Fabrice, I suppose.

MARGUERITE

No. You did.

ORNIFLE

I was very tired last night. I didn't know what I was saying. Don't you believe it, it's practically everything. Virtue's as common as daisies. It's beauty that is rare.

(*Shouting at* MLLE. SUPO.)

Supo, shut the window! I can't hear myself think with those little guttersnipes out there!

(MLLE. SUPO, *who has not taken her eyes off* MARGUERITE, *shuts the window and goes out, flooded by an awful presentiment.* ORNIFLE, *who had let slip his invalid pose, remembers to look slightly ill—not too much, just enough.*)

Unhappily for me, Fabrice's opinion has just been confirmed on all points by Dr. Galopin. Intermittent tachycardia, mitral stenosis, etc., etc. In short, everything the dear boy said. It's Bishop's disease all right, in its acute stage, diagnosed at sight. He's a very clever young man.

MARGUERITE

(*Beaming.*)

Yes, I know. I always said that Fabrice would be a great doctor.

ORNIFLE

Oh, there's no doubt of it now. He will be, bless him! A very great doctor indeed!

(*With a brave little smile.*)

I'm only sorry that I won't have the joy of seeing his success.

MARGUERITE

(*Impulsively, taking his hand.*)

The greatest doctors make mistakes, you know.

ORNIFLE

(*Patting her hand.*)

Very seldom. Galopin was speechless when I told him that Fabrice was only in his third year. He couldn't wait to congratulate him. I peeped through the door, but you were sleeping so soundly, both of you, I hadn't the heart to waken you.

MARGUERITE

(*Regretfully.*)

Oh, you should have. Fabrice would have been so proud.

ORNIFLE

(*Slyly.*)

I didn't like to. You looked so sweet there on the sofa, lying in each other's arms——

MARGUERITE

(*Blushing.*)

I already belong to Fabrice.

ORNIFLE

(*Smoothly.*)

And why not? You make a handsome couple, you are twenty years of age, you are in love. What else do you need, pray?

MARGUERITE

We would have had to wait a year, as it was, because of my father. And then Fabrice saw that he was going to have to kill his. There would have been no end of a delay. We decided to become man and wife first and postpone the ceremony until after the murder.

ORNIFLE

In other words, it was chiefly so as not to delay your wedding that you removed the bullets from the gun?

MARGUERITE

(*Hanging her head.*)

Yes. I must admit that I was mostly thinking of myself.

(*Looking up with a smile.*)

I didn't know you then, you see. Otherwise I might have thought of you a little too.

130

ORNIFLE

(*Gently.*)

There's no need to blush. It's a very good thing to think of oneself. Who said it wasn't? Fabrice again? If we didn't do it, who else would? God, when He put us on this earth, entrusted us with many things, but in particular with ourselves. We are our own little Providence and it's as well not to forget it. Look at the folk who only think of others, with their badly knotted ties and their neglected nails and their lank hair—how like waifs and strays they are!

MARGUERITE

(*Smiling.*)

I wish Fabrice could hear you!

ORNIFLE

I know. Fabrice thinks only of his duty. But that's only another way of thinking of yourself. If virtue did not give such joy to certain people, there would be far fewer men of duty, you may be sure of that.

(*Smiling.*)

But men of duty waken early. He'll be with us in a moment. Heaven knows when we'll have another chance to talk. Marguerite, I should like to make a pact with you.

MARGUERITE

(*Guardedly.*)

What sort of pact? We quarrel all the time, but I always tell Fabrice everything.

ORNIFLE

(*Two-faced.*)

I should hope so. A fine thing if you had secrets from each other!

(*Sighing.*)

But if it's for his own good . . . You know how slow he is at understanding. . . . If you tell him straightaway that I have spoken to you, there'll be no pact, that's all. Now, if you would help me persuade him . . . It wouldn't be a good deed exactly—I have a horror of good deeds—and I don't say it would be much fun. . . . But after all, you had decided to go and care for aborigines; and I know its a monstrous thing to say these days, but I'm as good as a black man.

MARGUERITE

Persuade him to do what? Why don't you say what you want to say?

ORNIFLE

(*With the irresistible air of an unhappy little boy.*)

I'm so afraid you may say No.

(*Taking the plunge.*)

It's like this. My doctors are quite emphatic about one thing. The time they have given me to live—which may be appreciably prolonged with luck and skillful nursing—will, in any case, be something of a feat. I shall have to go away, far from all worry. To the South, I imagine. The climate is supposed to be good for me—and I long for the sun. Persuade Fabrice to take me under his wing, and we'll all three go away together.

(*Smiling.*)

It shouldn't be too difficult. He's a stickler for duty.

MARGUERITE

But what about his studies?

ORNIFLE

We thought of that, Galopin and I. Machetu owns a large estate near Aix-en-Provence. He will be delighted to lend it to me. There is a famous medical school at Aix. Fabrice can continue his studies there and keep an eye on his sick father at the same time. Besides, for the year you have to spend away from Papa Pilu, it would be the ideal solution.

(*He sighs, the invalid again.*)

Either way, as you know, I shan't be with you for so very long.

MARGUERITE

(*After a short pause.*)

And what about me? What part do I play in all this?

ORNIFLE

(*Lyrical and utterly captivating.*)

You will complete the treatment. You will be the flower in my buttonhole, the young girl I never knew, in the guise of a clear-eyed little daughter-in-law. I have such a yearning for tenderness and purity! Yes, I want to try my hand at father roles! I can just see myself, with a panama hat, a stick maybe, going for easy walks——

MARGUERITE

(*Impulsively.*)

Oh, no!

ORNIFLE

(*Gratified by her exclamation, and feeling better already.*)

No. You're quite right. Come to think of it, I shall feel another ten years younger. That will make it twenty within a space of days. I'll be the same age as you then. It will be sheer heaven, you'll see. Together we'll explore the lovely countryside round Aix; we'll hunt for undiscovered Cézannes, while Fabrice, who doesn't care for modern painting anyway, attends his lectures. Sometimes we'll slip away somewhere—to the coast, perhaps, for a lobster lunch or a little dancing. Why not? If my physicians say I can. . . . I'm a very good dancer.

MARGUERITE

(*Sighing.*)

Fabrice doesn't approve of me dancing!

ORNIFLE

(*With old-world charm.*)

With his old father? Oh, come now. Why, it would be rather touching. I'll teach you the old-time waltzes.

(*Leaning toward her, conspiratorially.*)

Besides, we needn't tell him. . . . It would make me so happy to give you, purely out of selfishness, one or two of the innocent pleasures one is entitled to at your age, and which I'm sure he'll never give you. I shall be your young man Gaiety, and in the evening—when he comes back from school—you will find your young man Duty whom you love. Where's the woman who doesn't dream of such an arrangement? It will be the Garden of Eden—before the apple.

(*A pause.*)

Well? What do you say?

MARGUERITE

(*Gravely.*)

Yes. I accept, if I can be of any help to you. I'll speak to Fabrice.

ORNIFLE

Your hand to seal the bargain!

(*He kisses her hand very chastely.*)

Be clever. Young man Duty is a stickler for form.

MARGUERITE

(*Smiling conspiratorially.*)

What do you take me for? I know how to handle him. We fight like cat and dog, but he always does what I want in the end.

(*As an afterthought.*)

Only, in important things, I always see to it that the decisions appear to be his.

ORNIFLE

(*Beaming.*)

Bravo! I see there isn't much I have to teach you.

(*He gives her a merry wave of the hand as she trips out. Then he leaps out of bed, very debonair, and makes for the bathroom, singing at the top of his voice, "Jesu, you are hiding—tra-la-la." MLLE. SUPO has come in, gimlet-eyed.*)

Ah, Supo! Isn't life delicious! I can never understand how some fools can consent to die.

MLLE. SUPO

(*Braying.*)

I heard everything!

ORNIFLE

(*Over his shoulder.*)

You hear too much, my girl. You'll burst one day, with your ear at some strange keyhole.

(*He goes into the bathroom and reappears during the scene, shaving and dressing.*)

MLLE. SUPO

(*Bearing down on him.*)

You monster! You slimy hypocrite! I preferred you cynical, the way you were before, tumbling small-time actresses on your divan.

ORNIFLE

(*Reappearing.*)

Who told you that? So you don't just listen, you look through key-holes too?

MLLE. SUPO

(*Yelling.*)

Yes!

ORNIFLE

(*With genuine contempt, as he goes back into the bathroom.*)

Ignoble Supo!

MLLE. SUPO

Ignoble Supo has a soul, at least! And you are the devil incarnate!

ORNIFLE

(*Off.*)

Flatterer!

MLLE. SUPO

(*Striding to the door like an avenging Fury, and screeching.*)

You lied to that child! You mean to take ignominious advantage of an illness you know full well you haven't got! I can just see her, the virtuous little daughter-in-law, on the arm of her dewy-eyed papa, during those long chaste walks! I can see her, losing a little bit more ground each day; first surrendering her hand, as you help her over streams, then her bare arm . . . and then her thigh under her flimsy dress, a little too near yours on the rustic seat where lovers dream at night. . . . It will all seem so natural that she's the one who'll feel ashamed, at first, of thinking evil thoughts as she edges away. I can see her—I can see her now, part shy, part playful, allowing a sort of innocent convention to spring up between you, and then not daring to break it any more. I can see her shrinking back inside herself one day and going to her room, red-eyed. . . . And then, joining you later and relenting, to see you lying there so lonely and so ill—moved to pity, and vaguely flattered too, to have you at her feet like a pet poodle. And the other fool grinding away at his Anatomy and coming home late in the evenings, more and more rigid, less and less amusing.

I can see her right up till that late sultry afternoon—no longer very sure if she is happy or unhappy, if she will or she won't—when your hand—your foul, all-powerful hand—strays to forbidden places and pins her to the ground like a paralyzed gnat! I can see her waiting— as the blood pounds against her temples—for the inevitable to take its course, in horror or in rapture or in both! And then, the first occasion done, the first round lost, life will be all sweet simplicity. There will be nothing more to worry about then, save keeping the whole shabby business quiet!

ORNIFLE

(*Who has been listening with a faint smile playing on his lips, says coolly.*)
You have a point there, Supo. After your course of training at my keyholes, you have become clairvoyant. . . . Yes, I dare say that is what will happen. It will be very slow, and very difficult, but quite delicious.

MLLE. SUPO

But he's your son!

ORNIFLE

(*A shadow crosses his face, but he throws it off with a gesture.*)
Pah! He was never a real little boy. Too late now for paternal scruples. Let the fool defend his woman, if he can!
(*Calling.*)
Nenette!
(*Enter NENETTE.*)
Start packing. I leave for the South tonight. For several weeks. The young lady and gentleman will be staying to lunch.

NENETTE

Very good, sir.
(FABRICE *appears at the door.*)

ORNIFLE

What do *you* want?

FABRICE

I have just seen Marguerite. So I hadn't made a mistake, after all?

136

ORNIFLE

No. You hadn't made a mistake. I am going to kick off and you will become a famous doctor.

FABRICE

I came to tell you that my duty is plain. I will willingly undertake to look after you.

ORNIFLE

I shall make an impossible patient.

FABRICE

I know. But you can count on me, quite apart from the fact that you're my father. When I took up medicine, I vowed to make it a genuine vocation. I swore a solemn oath to Mother the night before I started medical school.

ORNIFLE

Another oath! Well, my boy, if you've a taste for dedication, I'm your man.

MLLE. SUPO

Stop! Stop! Stop!

ORNIFLE

Don't be alarmed, my dear boy. I live in the company of a hysteric. You can imagine how good that is for the heart. Go and find Marguerite. We leave tonight, all three of us—without, I may say, this madwoman here.

(FABRICE *goes out.*)

NENETTE

Mlle. Marie Pêche has called in on her way to the studio. She's downstairs. Shall I send her away?

ORNIFLE

(*After a brief hesitation.*)

Yes. . . . No. Dammit, life's too short. Show her into my sitting room.

NENETTE

(*Impassively.*)

The young couple are still in there.

ORNIFLE

(*Breezily.*)

True. No solecisms. . . . Tell her to wait for me next door, in the lobby of the Montesquieu Hotel. I'll join her.

(*He goes back into the bathroom.* MLLE. SUPO *rushes to the door and shouts.*)

MLLE. SUPO

God won't let you!

ORNIFLE

(*At the door, pulling on his shirt.*)

Men do a lot of things in spite of God! He won the first round. I have won the second. I know He'll win the rubber. He holds all the aces. But I'll have a run for my money!

(*He goes out, banging the door.*

MLLE. SUPO *is left in the middle of the room, standing very straight. She seems to be getting longer, scraggier, and her features take on a distorted, monstrous look. A storm begins to blow up outside and it grows rapidly darker.* NENETTE, *who has remained upstage, says simply.*)

NENETTE

Now don't take on so, Mlle. Supo. Men are men, and nothing you and I can do will change them.

(*She starts to strip the bed, takes the sheets to the window in order to air them, and leans out.*)

There he goes—frisky as a lad of seventeen! And not an hour ago he was thinking himself dead!

(MLLE. SUPO, *standing stiffly in the middle of the stage, begins to speak, while* NENETTE, *busy with her bedding, appears not to hear.*)

MLLE. SUPO

I'm sick of having a soul! They've never seen the real Supo. All they see of me is this great putty nose and my glasses and my dingy hair that's either straight as a rat's tail or frizzy with cheap permanents. All they can see are my dowdy frocks that fit me where they touch. All they see are the sea greens I laboriously match with mauves, the sunflower yellows with the cornflower blues. . . . And yet in the shop windows the colors gleam and sing, and I dream that I'll look beautiful. And when I appear in my homemade dress, they laugh.

(NENETTE *has hung out her bedding and goes out, without seeming to have heard.*

MLLE. SUPO *goes on tensely.*)

MLLE. SUPO

Yet, in my room, alone before the wardrobe mirror, naked, I am beautiful. My breasts are lovely and my belly round and hard; my legs are long and smooth from hours of loving care with wax and pumice—all for nothing.

(*Crying out suddenly, ludicrously pitiful.*)

Mlle. Supo is lovely as a seashell and no one has ever looked at her! Mlle. Supo is smooth and silky and no one has ever touched her! I am beautiful! Beautiful! Only my soul is ugly and stinks with all its murky crevices and narrow twisting ways. And it's my soul that makes my face!

(*It is almost dark. She stands very still in the gathering gloom. Then the telephone rings. She lets it ring for a moment or two, then answers it. Only the voice buzzing at the other end of the line breaks the silence.*

In her secretarial voice.)

Hello.

VOICE

Is that Monsieur Ornifle's residence?

MLLE. SUPO

It is.

VOICE

This is the manager of the Montesquieu Hotel here. Who is that speaking, please?

MLLE. SUPO

This is Monsieur Ornifle's private secretary.

VOICE

I am afraid I have bad news for you. There has been an accident. Would you be so good as to inform the family? Break it as gently as you can. As he came into the hotel lobby just now, Monsieur Ornifle was taken suddenly ill and collapsed. I had him carried into my office and a doctor who was on the premises gave him first aid—alas, too late. . . . I am most grieved to have to tell you. . . . It was his heart—I imagine you knew. Could you tell me what I am to do? Monsieur Ornifle is still in my office, but I shall have to make different arrangements very soon because of the hotel guests. I should like to have the family's instructions, as soon as possible, as to whether we should bring back Monsieur Ornifle's body in a taxi before registering the death, or whether we should notify the police ourselves and——

(MLLE. SUPO *has dropped the receiver. The voice continues to buzz incomprehensibly at the end of the line. She steps forward with an animal cry of anguish.*)

MLLE. SUPO

The body of Monsieur Ornifle!

(*She collapses sobbing on her master's bed and buries her head in his pajamas, which* NENETTE *has left there.*

Silence. Then the sky clears. A ray of sunshine lights up the window. Outside, the Institute CHILDREN *can be heard singing in heir high, thin voices.*)

CHILDREN

(*Off.*)

> Jesu, you are hiding,
> Jesu, where are you?
> I can see the kindly ox
> And the donkey too.

(MLLE. SUPO'*s sobbing, the voice buzzing on the line, and the Christmas carol blend in a strange harmony as the curtain falls.*)